GOLF RULES

ILLUSTRATED

Seventh Edition

COMPILED BY

THE ROYAL & ANCIENT GOLF CLUB
OF ST ANDREWS

Illustrations by Peter Davidson,
Terry McKivragan & Oxford Illustrators

HAMLYN

Foreword

It gives me great pleasure to write this foreword to the Seventh Edition of *Golf Rules Illustrated*.

The continuing worldwide increase in the popularity of golf and its exposure to the media has further stimulated interest in the Rules. Very frequently, this interest amounts to a fascination – even for those who have not yet played the game.

We hope that this New Edition, incorporating a changed format and additional illustrations, will provide useful guidance for everyone from the keenest student of the Rules to those embarking on the game for the first time.

JOHN S. SCRIVENER, Chairman
Rules of Golf Committee,
Royal & Ancient Golf Club of St. Andrews

Published in 1992
by The Hamlyn Publishing Group Limited
part of Reed International Books
Michelin House, 81 Fulham Road, London SW3 6RB

ISBN 0 600 57491 1

A catalogue record for this book is available from the British Library

Produced by Mandarin Offset
Printed in Hong Kong

Contents

SECTION I
ETIQUETTE

Courtesy on the Course

Safety

Prior to playing a stroke or making a practice swing, the player should ensure that no one is standing close by or in a position to be hit by the club, the ball or any stones, pebbles, twigs or the like which may be moved by the stroke or swing.

Consideration for Other Players

The player who has the honour should be allowed to play before his opponent or fellow-competitor tees his ball.

No one should move, talk or stand close to or directly behind the ball or the hole when a player is addressing the ball or making a stroke.

In the interest of all, players should play without delay.

No player should play until the players in front are out of range.

Players searching for a ball should signal the players behind them to pass as soon as it becomes apparent that the ball will not easily be found. They should not search for five minutes before doing so. They should not continue play until the players following them have passed and are out of range.

When the play of a hole has been completed, players should immediately leave the putting green.

Priority on the Course

In the absence of special rules, two-ball matches should have precedence over and be entitled to pass any three- or four-ball match, which should invite them through.

A single player has no standing and should give way to a match of any kind.

Any match playing a whole round is entitled to pass a match playing a shorter round.

If a match fails to keep its place on the course and loses more than one clear hole on the players in front, it should invite the match following to pass.

Care of the Course

Before leaving a bunker, a player should carefully fill up and smooth over all holes and footprints made by him.

Holes in Bunkers

Through the green, a player should ensure that any turf cut or displaced by him is replaced at once and pressed down and that any damage to the putting green made by a ball is carefully repaired. Damage to the putting green caused by golf shoe spikes should be repaired *on completion of the hole*.

Replace Divots; Repair Ball-Marks and Damage by Spikes

Players should ensure that, when putting down bags or the flagstick, no damage is done to the putting green and that neither they nor their caddies damage the hole by standing close to it, in handling the flagstick or in removing the ball from the hole. The flagstick should be properly replaced in the hole before the players leave the putting green. Players should not damage the putting green by leaning on their putters, particularly when removing the ball from the hole.

Damage to Greens - Flagsticks, Bags, etc.

Local notices regulating the movement of golf carts should be strictly observed.

Golf Carts

In taking practice swings, players should avoid causing damage to the course, particularly the tees, by removing divots.

Damage Through Practice Swings

Always repair divots. This is part of looking after the course (*top right*). Always carefully repair pitch marks on the putting green (*above*). Don't lean on your putter when you are removing the ball from the hole (*bottom right*).

SECTION II
DEFINITIONS

The Definitions are placed in alphabetical order and some are also repeated at the beginning of their relevant Rule.

In the Rules themselves, defined terms which may be important to the application of a Rule are emphasised in bold the first time they appear.

ADDRESSING THE BALL

Through the green a ball is addressed only when the player has taken his stance and the club is grounded.

In a bunker or other hazard, a ball is addressed when the player has taken his stance; the player must not ground the club.

The player is deliberately refraining from grounding his club, i.e. "addressing" the ball. If he grounded the club, and the wind then moved the ball, he would incur a penalty stroke.

Addressing the Ball

A player has "addressed the ball" when he has taken his **stance** and has also grounded his club, except that in a **hazard** a player has addressed the ball when he has taken his stance.

Advice

"Advice" is any counsel or suggestion which could influence a player in determining his play, the choice of a club or the method of making a **stroke**.

Information on the Rules or on matters of public information, such as the position of hazards or the flagstick on the putting green, is not advice.

Ball Deemed to Move

See " Move or Moved"

BALL DEEMED TO MOVE

This ball is deemed *not* to have "moved" because, having left its original position, it rolled back into it again.

This ball is deemed to have "moved" because it has left its original position and come to rest in another place; the fact that it has moved vertically, rather than laterally, is irrelevant.

Ball Holed

See "Holed"

Ball Lost

See " Lost Ball"

Ball in Play

A ball is "in play" as soon as the player has made a **stroke** on the **teeing ground**. It remains in play until holed out, except when it is **lost, out of bounds** or lifted, or another ball has been substituted under an applicable Rule, whether or not such Rule permits substitution; a ball so substituted becomes the ball in play.

Bunker

A "bunker" is a **hazard** consisting of a prepared area of ground, often a hollow, from which turf or soil has been removed and replaced with sand or the like. Grass-covered ground bordering or within a bunker is not part of the bunker. The margin of a bunker extends vertically downwards, but not upwards. *(Illustrated on page 8.)*

Caddie

A "caddie" is one who carries or handles a player's clubs during play and otherwise assists him in accordance with the Rules.

When one caddie is employed by more than one player, he is always deemed to be the caddie of the player whose ball is involved, and **equipment** carried by him is deemed to be that player's equipment, except when the caddie acts upon specific directions of another player, in which case he is considered to be that other player's caddie.

Casual Water

"Casual water" is any temporary accumulation of water on the **course** which is visible before or after the player takes his **stance** and is not in a **water hazard**. Snow and natural ice, other than frost, are either casual water or **loose impediments**, at the option of the player. Manufactured ice is an **obstruction**. Dew and frost are not casual water.

(Illustrated on page 9)

Committee

The "Committee" is the committee in charge of the competition or, if the matter does not arise in a competition, the committee in charge of the **course**.

Competitor

A "competitor" is a player in a stroke competition. A "fellow-competitor" is any person with whom the competitor plays. Neither is **partner** of the other.

In stroke play foursome and four-ball competitions, where the context so admits, the word "competitor" or "fellow-competitor" includes his partner.

Course

The "course" is the whole area within which play is permitted (see Rule 33-2).

Equipment

"Equipment" is anything used, worn or carried by or for the player except any ball he has played at the hole being played and any small object, such as a coin or a tee, when used to mark the position of a ball or the extent of an area in which a ball is to be dropped. Equipment includes a golf cart, whether or not motorised. If such a cart is shared by two or more players, the cart and everything in it are deemed to be the equipment of the player whose ball is involved except that, when the cart is being moved by one of the players sharing it, the cart and everything in it are deemed to be that player's equipment.

Note: A ball played at the hole being played is equipment when it has been lifted and not put back into play.

Fellow-Competitor

See " Competitor"

Flagstick

The "flagstick" is a movable straight indicator, with or without bunting or other material attached, centred in the hole to show its position. It shall be circular in cross-section.

BUNKER: GRASS ISLAND WITHIN BUNKER

A grass island within a bunker is not part of the bunker. The player may ground his club and remove loose impediments.

Forecaddie

A "forecaddie" is one who is employed by the Committee to indicate to players the position of balls during play. He is an **outside agency**.

Ground Under Repair

"Ground under repair" is any portion of the course so marked by order of the Committee or so declared by its authorised representative. It includes material piled for removal and a hole made by a greenkeeper, even if not so marked. Stakes and lines defining ground under repair are in such ground. The margin of ground under repair extends vertically downwards, but not upwards.

Note 1: Grass cuttings and other material left on

GROUND UNDER REPAIR

I am going to take a free drop here. These grass cuttings must be ground under repair.

No. Those grass cuttings have obviously been thrown under that bush to rot away. They can't be said to be ground under repair unless the Committee has marked them as such. You'll either have to play the ball as it lies or declare it unplayable.

the course which have been abandoned and are not intended to be removed are not ground under repair unless so marked.

Note 2: The Committee may make a Local Rule prohibiting play from ground under repair.

Hazards

A "hazard" is any **bunker** or **water hazard**.

Hole

The "hole" shall be 4¼ inches (108 mm) in diameter and at least 4 inches (100 mm) deep. If a lining is used, it shall be sunk at least 1 inch (25 mm) below the **putting green** surface unless the nature of the soil makes it impracticable to do so; its outer diameter shall not exceed 4¼ inches (108 mm).

Holed

A ball is "holed" when it is at rest within the circumference of the hole and all of it is below the level of the lip of the hole.

Honour

The side entitled to play first from the **teeing ground** is said to have the "honour".

Lateral Water Hazard

A "lateral water hazard" is a **water hazard** or that part of a water hazard so situated that it is not possible or is deemed by the Committee to be impracticable to drop a ball behind the water hazard in accordance with Rule 26-1b.

That part of a water hazard to be played as a lateral water hazard should be distinctively marked.

Note: Lateral water hazards should be defined by red stakes or lines.

Line of Play

The "line of play" is the direction which the player wishes his ball to take after a stroke, plus a reasonable distance on either side of the intended direction. The line of play extends vertically upwards from the ground, but does not extend beyond the hole.

Line of Putt

The "line of putt" is the line which the player wishes his ball to take after a stroke on the **putting green**. Except with respect to Rule 16-1e, the line of putt includes a reasonable distance on either side of the intended line. The line of putt does not extend beyond the hole.

Loose Impediments

"Loose impediments" are natural objects such as stones, leaves, twigs, branches and the like, dung, worms and insects and casts or heaps made by them, provided they are not fixed or growing, are not solidly embedded and do not adhere to the ball.

Sand and loose soil are loose impediments on the **putting green**, but not elsewhere.

Snow and natural ice, other than frost, are either **casual water** or loose impediments, at the option of the player. Manufactured ice is an **obstruction**.

Dew and frost are not loose impediments.

Lost Ball

A ball is "lost" if:

a. It is not found or identified as his by the player within five minutes after the player's side or his or their caddies have begun to search for it; or

b. The player has put another ball into play under the Rules, even though he may not have searched for the original ball; or

c. The player has played any stroke with a **provisional ball** from the place where the original ball is likely to be or from a point nearer the hole than that place, whereupon the provisional ball becomes the **ball in play**.

Time spent in playing a **wrong ball** is not counted in the five-minute period allowed for search.

Marker

A "marker" is one who is appointed by the Committee to record a **competitor's** score in

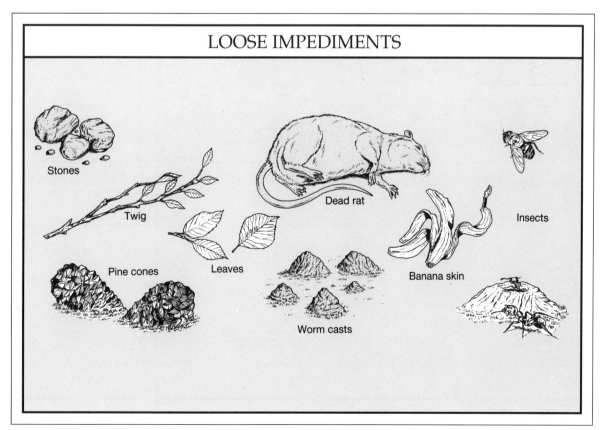

LOOSE IMPEDIMENTS

Stones

Twig

Pine cones

Leaves

Dead rat

Worm casts

Banana skin

Insects

stroke play. He may be a **fellow-competitor**. He is not a **referee**.

Matches

See "Sides and Matches".

Move or Moved

A ball is deemed to have "moved" if it leaves its position and comes to rest in any other place.

Observer

An "observer" is one who is appointed by the Committee to assist a **referee** to decide questions of fact and to report to him any breach of a Rule. An observer should not attend the flagstick, stand at or mark the position of the hole, or lift the ball or mark its position.

Obstructions

An "obstruction" is anything artificial, including the artificial surfaces and sides of roads and paths and manufactured ice, except:

a. Objects defining **out of bounds**, such as walls, fences, stakes and railings;

b. Any part of an immovable artificial object which is out of bounds; and

c. Any construction declared by the Committee to be an integral part of the course.

Out of Bounds

"Out of bounds" is ground on which play is prohibited.

When out of bounds is defined by reference to stakes or a fence or as being beyond stakes or a fence, the out of bounds line is determined by the nearest inside points of the stakes or fence posts at ground level excluding angled supports.

When out of bounds is defined by a line on the ground, the line itself is out of bounds.

The out of bounds line extends vertically upwards and downwards.

A ball is out of bounds when all of it lies out

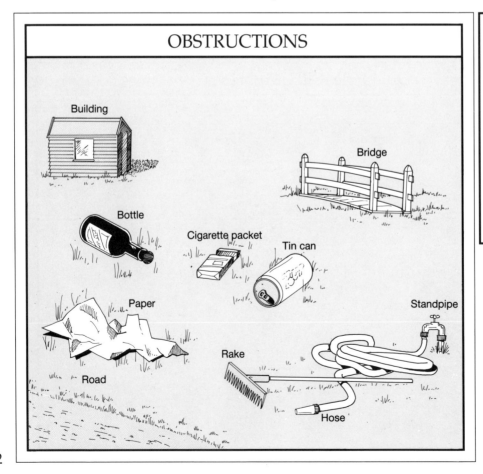

OBSTRUCTIONS

Building

Bridge

Bottle

Cigarette packet

Tin can

Paper

Standpipe

Rake

Road

Hose

Right: **Out of bounds**
(**a**) - (**c**): The out of bounds line is the dotted line. All of the ball must lie beyond this line for it to be out of bounds.
(**d**): A ball in or beyond the trench is out of bounds.
(**e**) - (**f**): The line itself is out of bounds. Therefore, the ball on the left is in bounds and the ball on the right is out of bounds.

of bounds.

A player may stand out of bounds to play a ball lying within bounds.

Outside Agency

An "outside agency" is any agency not part of the match or, in stroke play, not part of the competitor's side, and includes a referee, a marker, an observer or a forecaddie.

Neither wind nor water is an outside agency.

Partner

A "partner" is a player associated with another player on the same side.

In a threesome, foursome, best-ball or four-ball match, where the context so admits, the word "player" includes his partner or partners.

Penalty Stroke

A "penalty stroke" is one added to the score of a player or **side** under certain Rules. In a threesome

or foursome, penalty strokes do not affect the order of play.

Provisional Ball

A "provisional ball" is a ball played under Rule 27-2 for a ball which may be **lost** outside a **water hazard** or may be **out of bounds**.

Putting Green

The "putting green" is all ground of the hole being played which is specially prepared for putting or otherwise defined as such by the Committee. A ball is on the putting green when any part of it touches the putting green.

Referee

A "referee" is one who is appointed by the Committee to accompany players to decide questions of fact and apply the Rules of Golf. He shall act on any breach of a Rule which he observes or is reported to him.

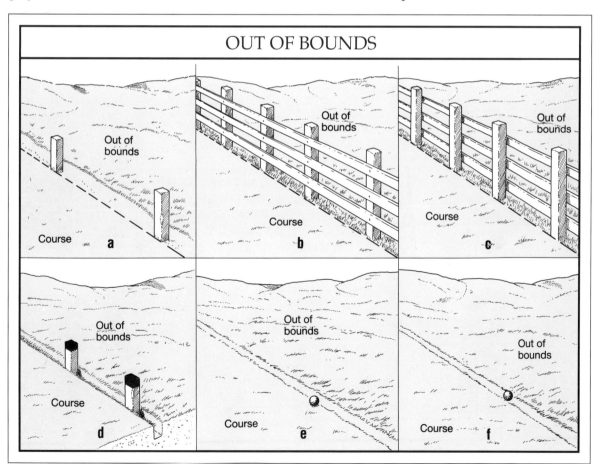

OUT OF BOUNDS

A referee should not attend the flagstick, stand at or mark the position of the hole, or lift the ball or mark its position.

Rub of the Green

A "rub of the green" occurs when a ball in motion is accidentally deflected or stopped by any **outside agency** (see Rule 19-1).

Rule

The term "Rule" includes Local Rules made by the Committee under Rule 33-8a.

Sides and Matches

Side: A player, or two or more players who are **partners**.

Single: A match in which one plays against another.

Threesome: A match in which one plays against two, and each side plays one ball.

Foursome: A match in which two play against two, and each side plays one ball.

Three-ball: A match play competition in which three play against one another, each playing his own ball. Each player is playing two distinct matches.

Best-ball: A match in which one plays against the better ball of two or the best ball of three players.

Four-ball: A match in which two play their better ball against the better ball of two other players.

Stance

Taking the "stance" consists in a player placing his feet in position for and preparatory to making a **stroke**.

Stipulated Round

The "stipulated round" consists of playing the holes of the course in their correct sequence unless otherwise authorised by the Committee. The number of holes in a stipulated round is 18 unless a smaller number is authorised by the Committee. As to extension of stipulated round in match play, see Rule 2-3.

STIPULATED ROUND: SUDDEN DEATH PLAY-OFF

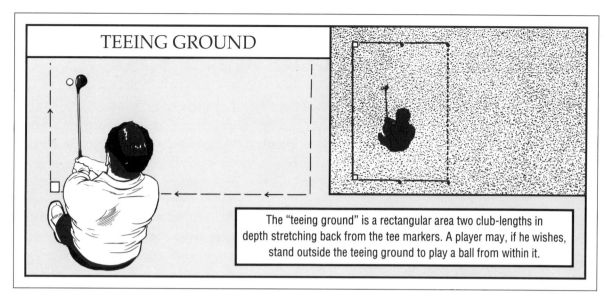

TEEING GROUND

The "teeing ground" is a rectangular area two club-lengths in depth stretching back from the tee markers. A player may, if he wishes, stand outside the teeing ground to play a ball from within it.

Stroke

A "stroke" is the forward movement of the club made with the intention of fairly striking at and moving the ball, but if a player checks his downswing voluntarily before the clubhead reaches the ball he is deemed not to have made a stroke.

Teeing Ground

The "teeing ground" is the starting place for the hole to be played. It is a rectangular area two club-lengths in depth, the front and the sides of which are defined by the outside limits of two tee-markers. A ball is outside the teeing ground when all of it lies outside the teeing ground.

Through the Green

"Through the green" is the whole area of the **course** except:

a. The **teeing ground** and **putting green** of the hole being played; and

b. All **hazards** on the course.

Water Hazard

A "water hazard" is any sea, lake, pond, river, ditch, surface drainage ditch or other open water course (whether or not containing water) and anything of a similar nature.

All ground or water within the margin of a water hazard is part of the water hazard. The margin of a water hazard extends vertically upwards and downwards. Stakes and lines defining the margins of water hazards are in the hazards.

Note: Water hazards (other than **lateral water hazards**) should be defined by yellow stakes or lines.

Wrong Ball

A "wrong ball" is any ball other than:

a. The **ball in play**,

b. A **provisional ball** or

c. In stroke play, a second ball played under Rule 3-3 or Rule 20-7b.

Note: Ball in play includes a ball substituted for the ball in play when the player is proceeding under an applicable Rule which does not permit substitution.

SECTION III
THE RULES OF PLAY

THE GAME

Rule 1-1   General

The Game of Golf consists in playing a ball from the **teeing ground** into the hole by a **stroke** or successive strokes in accordance with the Rules.

Rule 1-2   Exerting Influence on Ball

No player or caddie shall take any action to influence the position or the movement of a ball except in accordance with the Rules.

PENALTY FOR BREACH OF RULE 1-2: *Match Play — Loss of hole; Stroke play — Two strokes.*

Note: In the case of a serious breach of Rule 1-2, the Committee may impose a penalty of disqualification.

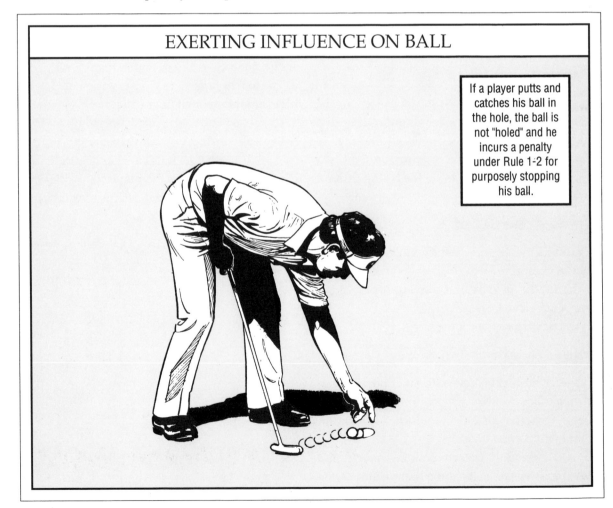

EXERTING INFLUENCE ON BALL

If a player putts and catches his ball in the hole, the ball is not "holed" and he incurs a penalty under Rule 1-2 for purposely stopping his ball.

Agreement to Waive Rules   Rule 1-3

Players shall not agree to exclude the operation of any Rule or to waive any penalty incurred.

PENALTY FOR BREACH OF RULE 1-3: *Match play — Disqualification of both sides; Stroke play — Disqualification of competitors concerned.*

(Agreeing to play out of turn in stroke play — see Rule 10-2c.)

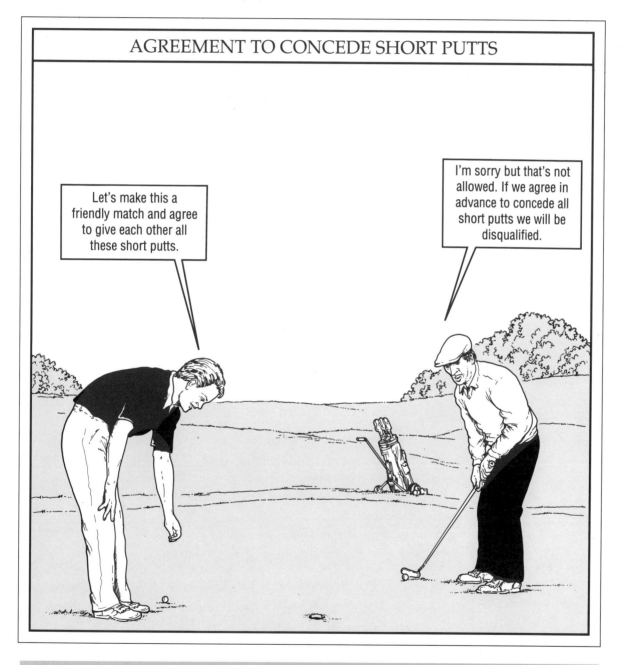

AGREEMENT TO CONCEDE SHORT PUTTS

Let's make this a friendly match and agree to give each other all these short putts.

I'm sorry but that's not allowed. If we agree in advance to concede all short putts we will be disqualified.

Points Not Covered by Rules   Rule 1-4

If any point in dispute is not covered by the Rules, the decision shall be made in accordance with equity.

MATCH PLAY

| Rule 2-1 | **Winner of Hole; Reckoning of Holes** |

In match play the game is played by holes.

Except as otherwise provided in the Rules, a hole is won by the side which holes its ball in the fewer strokes. In a handicap match the lower net score wins the hole.

The reckoning of holes is kept by the terms: so many "holes up" or "all square", and so many "to play".

A side is "dormie" when it is as many holes up as there are holes remaining to be played.

| Rule 2-2 | **Halved Hole** |

A hole is halved if each side holes out in the same number of strokes.

When a player has holed out and his opponent has been left with a stroke for the half, if the player thereafter incurs a penalty, the hole is halved.

| Rule 2-3 | **Winner of Match** |

A match (which consists of a **stipulated round**, unless otherwise decreed by the Committee) is won by the side which is leading by a number of holes greater than the number of holes remaining to be played.

The Committee may, for the purpose of settling a tie, extend the stipulated round to as many holes as are required for a match to be won.

| Rule 2-4 | **Concession of Next Stroke, Hole or Match** |

When the opponent's ball is at rest or is deemed to be at rest under Rule 16-2, the player may concede the opponent to have holed out with his next stroke and the ball may be removed by either side with a club or otherwise.

A player may concede a hole or a match at any time prior to the conclusion of the hole or the match.

Concession of a stroke, hole or match may not be declined or withdrawn.

| Rule 2-5 | **Claims** |

In match play, if a doubt or dispute arises between the players and no duly authorised representative of the Committee is available within a reasonable time, the players shall continue the match without delay. Any claim, if it is to be considered by the Committee, must be made before any player in the match plays from the next teeing ground or, in the case of the last hole of the match, before all players in the match leave the putting green.

No later claim shall be considered unless it is based on facts previously unknown to the player making the claim and the player making the claim had been given wrong information (Rules 6-2a and 9) by an opponent. In any case, no later claim shall be considered after the result of the match has been officially announced, unless the Committee is satisfied that the opponent knew he was giving wrong information.

General Penalty   Rule 2-6

The penalty for a breach of a Rule in match play is loss of hole, except when otherwise provided.

STROKE PLAY

Winner   Rule 3-1

The competitor who plays the **stipulated round** or rounds in the fewest strokes is the winner.

Failure to Hole Out   Rule 3-2

If a competitor fails to hole out at any hole and does not correct his mistake before he plays a **stroke** from the next **teeing ground** or, in the case of the last hole of the round, before he leaves the **putting green**, *he shall be disqualified.*

Doubt as to Procedure   Rule 3-3

a *Procedure*

In stroke play only, when during play of a hole a competitor is doubtful of his rights or procedure, he may, without penalty, play a second ball. After the situation which caused the doubt has arisen, the competitor should, before taking further action, announce to his marker or a fellow-competitor his decision to invoke this Rule and the ball with which he will score if the Rules permit.

The competitor shall report the facts to the **Committee** before returning his score card unless he scores the same with both balls; if he fails to do so, *he shall be disqualified.*

b *Determination of Score for Hole*

If the Rules allow the procedure selected in advance by the competitor, the score with the ball selected shall be his score for the hole.

If the competitor fails to announce in advance his decision to invoke this Rule or his selection, the score with the original ball or, if the original ball is not one of the balls being played, the first ball put into play shall count if the Rules allow the procedure adopted for such ball.

Note: A second ball played under Rule 3-3 is not a provisional ball under Rule 27-2.

Refusal to Comply with a Rule   Rule 3-4

If a competitor refuses to comply with a Rule affecting the rights of another competitor, *he shall be disqualified.*

DOUBT AS TO PROCEDURE IN STROKE PLAY

I'm not sure whether I can get free relief from this path. As it's stroke play I'll play out the hole with two balls, this ball as it lies, and then another ball having taken a drop away from the path. I would like the second ball to count, if the Rule permits.

That's fine. I'll put the scores for both balls on your card and we'll get a decision from the Committee when we get in.

Rule 3-5   **General Penalty**

The penalty for a breach of a Rule in stroke play is two strokes except when otherwise provided.

CLUBS AND THE BALL

The Royal and Ancient Golf Club of St. Andrews and the United States Golf Association reserve the right to change the Rules and make and change the interpretations relating to clubs, balls and other implements at any time.

CLUBS

If there may be any reasonable basis for doubt as to whether a club which is to be manufactured conforms with Rule 4 and Appendix II the manufacturer should submit a sample to the Royal and Ancient Golf Club of St. Andrews for a ruling, such sample to become its property for reference purposes. If a manufacturer fails to do so, he assumes the risk of a ruling that the club does not conform with the Rules of Golf.

A player in doubt as to the conformity of a club should consult the Royal and Ancient Golf Club of St. Andrews.

A club is an implement designed to be used for striking the ball. A putter is a club designed primarily for use on the putting green. The player's clubs shall conform with the provisions of this Rule and with the specifications and interpretations set forth in Appendix II

The club shall be composed of a shaft and a head. All parts of the club shall be fixed so that the club is one unit. The club shall not be designed to be adjustable except for weight (see also Appendix II). The club shall not be substantially different from the traditional and customary form and make.

a *General*

The shaft shall be generally straight, with the same bending and twisting properties in any direction, and shall be attached to the clubhead at the heel either directly or through a single plain neck or socket. A putter shaft may be attached to any point in the head.

b *Shaft*

The grip consists of that part of the shaft designed to be held by the player and any material added to it for the purpose of obtaining a firm hold. The grip shall be substantially straight and plain in form and shall not be moulded for any part of the hands.

c *Grip*

The distance from the heel to the toe of the clubhead shall be greater than the distance from the face to the back. The clubhead shall be generally plain in shape. The clubhead shall have only one face designed for striking the ball, except that a putter may have two such faces if their characteristics are the same, they are opposite each other and the loft of each is the same and does not exceed ten degrees.

d *Clubhead*

The face shall not have any degree of concavity and, in relation to the ball, shall be hard and rigid. It shall be generally smooth except for such markings as are permitted by Appendix II.

e *Club Face*

A club which conforms with Rule 4-1 when new is deemed to conform after wear through normal use. Any part of a club which has been purposely altered is regarded as new and must conform, in the altered state, with the Rules.

f *Wear*

If a player's club ceases to conform with Rule 4-1 because of damage sustained in the normal course of play, the player may:
(i)   use the club in its damaged state, but only for the remainder of the **stipulated round** during which such damage was sustained; or
(ii) without unduly delaying play, repair it.
  A club which ceases to conform because of damage sustained other than in the normal course of play shall not subsequently be used during the round.
  (Damage changing playing characteristics of club – see Rule 4-2.)
  (Damage rendering club unfit for play – see Rule 4-4a.)

g *Damage*

Rule 4-2   Playing Characteristics Changed

During a **stipulated round**, the playing characteristics of a club shall not be purposely changed by adjustment or by any other means.

If the playing characteristics of a player's club are changed during a round because of damage sustained in the normal course of play, the player may:

(i)   use the club in its altered state; or

(ii)   without unduly delaying play, repair it.

If the playing characteristics of a player's club are changed because of damage sustained other than in the normal course of play, the club shall not subsequently be used during the round.

Damage to a club which occurred prior to a round may be repaired during the round, provided the playing characteristics are not changed and play is not unduly delayed.

Rule 4-3   Foreign Material

No foreign material shall be applied to the club face for the purpose of influencing the movement of the ball.

PENALTY FOR BREACH OF RULE 4-1, -2 or -3: *Disqualification.*

Rule 4-4   Maximum of Fourteen Clubs

a *Selection and Replacement of Clubs*

The player shall start a **stipulated round** with not more than fourteen clubs. He is limited to the clubs thus selected for that round except that, without unduly delaying play, he may:

(i)   if he started with fewer than fourteen, add as many as will bring his total to that number; and

(ii)   replace, with any club, a club which becomes unfit for play in the normal course of play.

The addition or replacement of a club or clubs may not be made by borrowing any club selected for play by any other person playing on the course.

Partners may share clubs, provided that the total number of clubs carried by the partners so sharing does not exceed fourteen.

b *Partners May Share Clubs*

PENALTY FOR BREACH OF RULE 4-4a or b, REGARDLESS OF NUMBER OF EXCESS CLUBS CARRIED: *Match play — At the conclusion of the hole at which the breach is discovered, the state of the match shall be adjusted by deducting one hole for each hole at which a breach occurred. Maximum deduction per round: two holes.*
Stroke play — Two strokes for each hole at which any breach occurred; maximum penalty per round: four strokes.
Bogey and par competitions — Penalties as in match play.
Stableford competitions — see Note to Rule 32-1b.

Any club carried or used in breach of this Rule shall be declared out of play by the player immediately upon discovery that a breach has occurred and thereafter shall not be used by the player during the round.

c *Excess Club Declared Out of Play*

PENALTY FOR BREACH OF RULE 4-4c: *Disqualification.*

THE BALL

Rule 5-1   General

The ball the player uses shall conform to specifications set forth in Appendix III on maximum weight, minimum size, spherical symmetry, initial velocity and overall distance when tested under specified conditions.

Note: In laying down the conditions under which a competition is to be played (Rule 33-1), the Committee may stipulate that the ball to be used shall be of certain specifications, provided these specifications are within the limits prescribed by Appendix III, and that it be of a brand and marking as detailed on the current List of Conforming Golf Balls issued by the Royal and Ancient Golf Club of St. Andrews.

Rule 5-2   Foreign Material

No foreign material shall be applied to a ball for the purpose of changing its playing characteristics.

PENALTY FOR BREACH OF RULE 5-1 or 5-2: *Disqualification.*

Rule 5-3   Ball Unfit for Play

A ball is unfit for play if it is visibly cut, cracked or out of shape. A ball is not unfit for play solely because mud or other materials adhere to it, its surface is scratched or scraped or its paint is damaged or discoloured.

If a player has reason to believe his ball has become unfit for play during the play of the hole being played, he may during the play of such hole lift his ball without penalty to determine whether it is unfit.

Before lifting the ball, the player must announce his intention to his opponent in match play or his marker or a fellow-competitor in stroke play and mark the position of the ball. He may then lift and examine the ball without cleaning it and must give his opponent, marker or fellow-competitor an opportunity to examine the ball.

If he fails to comply with this procedure, *he shall incur a penalty of one stroke.*

If it is determined that the ball has become unfit for play during play of the hole being played, the player may substitute another ball, placing it on the spot where the original ball lay. Otherwise, the original ball shall be replaced.

If a ball breaks into pieces as a result of a stroke, the stroke shall be cancelled and the player shall play a ball without penalty as nearly as possible at the spot from which the original ball was played (see Rule 20-5).

PENALTY FOR BREACH OF RULE 5-3: *Match play — Loss of hole; Stroke play — Two strokes.*

If a player incurs the general penalty for breach of Rule 5-3, no additional penalty under the Rule shall be applied.

Note: If the opponent, marker or fellow-competitor wishes to dispute a claim of unfitness, he must do so before the player plays another ball.

(Cleaning ball lifted from putting green or under any other Rule – see Rule 21.)

The player is responsible for knowing the conditions under which the competition is to be played (Rule 33-1).

THE PLAYER

Definition

A *"marker" is one who is appointed by the Committee to record a* **competitor's** *score in stroke play. He may be a* **fellow-competitor**. *He is not a* **referee**.

Conditions of Competition **Rule 6-1**

The player is responsible for knowing the conditions under which the competition is to be played (Rule 33-1).

Rule 6-2   Handicap

a *Match Play*

Before starting a match in a handicap competition, the players should determine from one another their respective handicaps. If a player begins the match having declared a higher handicap which would affect the number of strokes given or received, *he shall be disqualified*; otherwise, the player shall play off the declared handicap.

b *Stroke Play*

In any round of a handicap competition, the competitor shall ensure that his handicap is recorded on his score card before it is returned to the Committee. If no handicap is recorded on his score card before it is returned, or if the recorded handicap is higher than that to which he is entitled and this affects the number of strokes received, *he shall be disqualified* from that round of the handicap competition; otherwise, the score shall stand.

Note: It is the player's responsibility to know the holes at which handicap strokes are to be given or received.

Rule 6-3   Time of Starting and Groups

a *Time of Starting*

The player shall start at the time laid down by the Committee.

b *Groups*

In stroke play, the competitor shall remain throughout the round in the group arranged by the Committee unless the Committee authorises or ratifies a change.

PENALTY FOR BREACH OF RULE 6-3: *Disqualification.*

(Best-ball and four-ball play — see Rules 30-3a and 31-2.)

Note: The Committee may provide in the conditions of a competition (Rule 33-1) that, if the player arrives at his starting point, ready to play, within five minutes after his starting time, in the absence of circumstances which warrant waiving the penalty of disqualification as provided in Rule 33-7, the penalty for failure to start on time is *loss of the first hole in match play or two strokes at the first hole in stroke play* instead of disqualification.

Rule 6-4   Caddie

The player may have only one **caddie** at any one time, *under penalty of disqualification.*

     For any breach of a Rule by his caddie, the player incurs the applicable penalty.

Rule 6-5   Ball

The responsibility for playing the proper ball rests with the player. Each player should put an identification mark on his ball.

Rule 6-6   Scoring in Stroke Play

a *Recording Scores*

After each hole the **marker** hould check the score with the competitor and record it. On completion of the round the marker shall sign the card and hand it to the competitor. If more than one marker records the scores, each shall sign for the part for which he is responsible.

After completion of the round, the competitor should check his score for each hole and settle any doubtful points with the Committee. He shall ensure that the marker has signed the card, countersign the card himself and return it to the Committee as soon as possible.

b *Signing and Returning Card*

PENALTY FOR BREACH OF RULE 6-6b: *Disqualification*.

No alteration may be made on a card after the competitor has returned it to the Committee.

c *Alteration of Card*

The competitor is responsible for the correctness of the score recorded for each hole. If he returns a score for any hole lower than actually taken, *he shall be disqualified*. If he returns a score for any hole higher than actually taken, the score as returned shall stand.

d *Wrong Score for Hole*

Note 1: The Committee is responsible for the addition of scores and application of the handicap recorded on the card — see Rule 33-5.
Note 2: In four-ball stroke play, see also Rule 31-4 and -7a.

Rule 6-7   Undue Delay

The player shall play without undue delay. Between completion of a hole and playing from the next teeing ground, the player shall not unduly delay play.

PENALTY FOR BREACH OF RULE 6-7: *Match play — Loss of hole; Stroke play — Two Strokes. For repeated offence — Disqualification.*

If the player unduly delays play between holes, he is delaying the play of the next hole and the penalty applies to that hole.

Rule 6-8   Discontinuance of Play

a *When Permitted*   The player shall not discontinue play unless:

(i)   the Committee has suspended play;

(ii)   he believes there is danger from lightning;

(iii)   he is seeking a decision from the Committee on a doubtful or disputed point (see Rules 2-5 and 34-3); or

(iv)   there is some other good reason such as sudden illness.

      Bad weather is not of itself a good reason for discontinuing play.

If the player discontinues play without specific permission from the Committee, he shall report to the Committee as soon as practicable. If he does so and the Committee considers his reason satisfactory, the player incurs no penalty. Otherwise, *the player shall be disqualified.*

Exception in match play: Players discontinuing match play by agreement are not subject to disqualification unless by so doing the competition is delayed.

Note: Leaving the course does not of itself constitute discontinuance of play.

When play is suspended by the Committee, if the players in a match or group are between the play of two holes, they shall not resume play until the Committee has ordered a resumption of play. If they are in the process of playing a hole, they may continue provided they do so without delay. If they choose to continue, they shall discontinue either before or immediately after completing the hole, and shall not thereafter resume play until the Committee has ordered a resumption of play.

b *Procedure When Play Suspended by Committee*

When play has been suspended by the Committee, the player shall resume play when the Committee has ordered a resumption of play.

PENALTY FOR BREACH OF RULE **6-8b**: *Disqualification.*

When during the play of a hole a player discontinues play under Rule 6-8a, he may lift his ball. A ball may be cleaned when so lifted. If a ball has been so lifted, the player shall, when play is resumed, place a ball on the spot from which the original ball was lifted.

c *Lifting Ball When Play Discontinued*

PENALTY FOR BREACH OF RULE **6-8c:** *Match play — Loss of hole; Stroke play — Two strokes.*

PRACTICE

| Rule 7-1 | Before or Between Rounds |

a *Match Play*

On any day of a match play competition, a player may practise on the competition **course** before a round.

b *Stroke Play*

On any day of a stroke competition or play-off, a competitor shall not practise on the competition **course** or test the surface of any putting green on the course before a round or play-off. When two or more rounds of a stroke competition are to be played over consecutive days, practice between those rounds on any competition course remaining to be played is prohibited.

Exception: Practice putting or chipping on or near the first **teeing ground** before starting a round or play-off is permitted.

PENALTY FOR BREACH OF RULE 7-1b: *Disqualification*.

Note: The Committee may in the conditions of a competition (Rule 33-1) prohibit practice on the competition course on any day of a match play competition or permit practice on the competition course or part of the course (Rule 33-2c) on any day of or between rounds of a stroke competition.

| Rule 7-2 | During Round |

A player shall not play a practice **stroke** either during the play of a hole or between the play of two holes except that, between the play of two holes, the player may practise putting or chipping on or near the **putting green** of the hole last played, any practice putting green or the **teeing ground** of the next hole to be played in the round, provided such practice stroke is not played from a hazard and does not unduly delay play (Rule 6-7).

Exception: When play has been suspended by the Committee, a player may, prior to resumption of play, practise (a) as provided in this Rule, (b) anywhere other than on the competition course and (c) as otherwise permitted by the Committee.

> Practice putting and chipping on or near the tee of the next hole to be played is permitted as long as play is not delayed.

PENALTY FOR BREACH OF RULE 7-2: *Match play — Loss of hole: Stroke play — Two strokes.*
In the event of a breach between the play of two holes, the penalty applies to the next hole.
Note 1: A practice swing is not a practice **stroke** and may be taken at any place,
provided the player does not breach the Rules.
Note 2: The Committee may prohibit practice on or near the **putting green** of the
hole last played.

ADVICE; INDICATING LINE OF PLAY

Definitions

*"Advice" is any counsel or suggestion which could influence a player in
determining his play, the choice of a club or the method of making a* **stroke**.

*Information on the Rules or on matters of public information, such as the
position of hazards or the flagstick on the putting green, is not advice.*

*The "line of play" is the direction which the player wishes his ball to take
after a stroke, plus a reasonable distance on either side of the intended direction.
The line of play extends vertically upwards from the ground, but does not extend
beyond the hole.*

Advice   Rule 8-1

A player shall not give **advice** to anyone in the competition except his partner.
A player may ask for advice from only his partner or either of their caddies.

My yardage chart shows that I have 150 yards to go to the green from this bunker. I can use this information because distance charts are permissible under the Rules.

Yes of course. But if you had asked me what club to use you would have been penalised for seeking advice.

Rule 8-2   Indicating Line of Play

a *Other Than on Putting Green*

Except on the **putting green**, a player may have the **line of play** indicated to him by anyone, but no one shall stand on or close to the line while the **stroke** is being played. Any mark placed during the play of a hole by the player or with his knowledge to indicate the line shall be removed before the stroke is played. *Exception:* Flagstick attended or held up – see Rule 17-1.

b *On the Putting Green*

When the player's ball is on the **putting green**, the player, his partner or either of their caddies may, before but not during the **stroke**, point out a line for putting, but in so doing the putting green shall not be touched. No mark shall be placed anywhere to indicate a line for putting.

PENALTY FOR BREACH OF RULE: *Match play – Loss of hole: Stroke play – Two strokes.*
Note: In a team competition with or without concurrent individual competition, the Committee may in the conditions of the competition (Rule 33-1) permit each team to appoint one person, e.g. team captain or coach, who may give **advice** (including pointing out a line for putting) to members of that team. Such person shall be identified to the Committee prior to the start of the competition.

On the putting green, the player, his caddie, his partner or his partner's caddie may point out a line for putting.

I am going to putt this. I know that I can't place a mark on the green to give me a line but may I make a mark off the green?

No. You would lose the hole in match play or incur a penalty of two strokes in stroke play if you placed a mark to indicate the line and played a stroke before removing the mark.

9

INFORMATION AS TO STROKES TAKEN

General   **Rule 9-1**

The number of strokes a player has taken shall include any penalty strokes incurred.

Match Play   **Rule 9-2**

A player who has incurred a penalty shall inform his opponent as soon as practicable, unless he is obviously proceeding under a Rule involving a penalty and this has been observed by his opponent. If he fails so to inform his opponent, he shall be deemed to have given wrong information, even if he was not aware that he had incurred a penalty.

An opponent is entitled to ascertain from the player, during the play of a hole, the number of strokes he has taken and, after play of a hole, the number of strokes taken on the hole just completed.

If during the play of a hole the player gives or is deemed to give wrong information as to the number of strokes taken, he shall incur no penalty if he corrects the mistake before his opponent has played his next stroke. If the player fails so to correct the wrong information, *he shall lose the hole.*

If after play of a hole the player gives or is deemed to give wrong information as to the number of strokes taken on the hole just completed and this affects the opponent's understanding of the result of the hole, he shall incur no penalty if he corrects his mistake before any player plays from the next **teeing ground** or, in the case of the last hole of the match, before all players leave the **putting green**. If the player fails so to correct the wrong information, he shall lose the hole.

Stroke Play   **Rule 9-3**

A competitor who has incurred a penalty should inform his marker as soon as practicable.

10

ORDER OF PLAY

Match Play   **Rule 10-1**

The side entitled to play first from the **teeing ground** is said to have the "honour".   **a** *Teeing Ground*

The side which shall have the honour at the first teeing ground shall be determined by the order of the draw. In the absence of a draw, the honour

33

should be decided by lot.

The side which wins a hole shall take the honour at the next teeing ground. If a hole has been halved, the side which had the honour at the previous teeing ground shall retain it.

b *Other Than on Teeing Ground*

When the balls are in play, the ball farther from the hole shall be played first. If the balls are equidistant from the hole, the ball to be played first should be decided by lot. *Exception*: Rule 30-3c (best-ball and four-ball match play).

c *Playing Out of Turn*

If a player plays when his opponent should have played, the opponent may immediately require the player to cancel the stroke so played and, in correct order, play a ball without penalty as nearly as possible at the spot from which the original ball was last played (see Rule 20-5).

Rule 10-2   Stroke Play

a *Teeing Ground*

The competitor entitled to play first from the **teeing ground** is said to have the "honour".

The competitor who shall have the honour at the first teeing ground shall be determined by the order of the draw. In the absence of a draw, the honour should be decided by lot.

The competitor with the lowest score at a hole shall take the honour at the next teeing ground. The competitor with the second lowest score shall play next and so on. If two or more competitors have the same score at a hole, they shall play from the next teeing ground in the same order as at the previous teeing ground.

b *Other Than on the Teeing Ground*

When the balls are in play, the ball farthest from the hole shall be played first. If two or more balls are equidistant from the hole, the ball to be played first should be decided by lot.

Exceptions: Rules 22 (ball interfering with or assisting play) and 31-5 (four-ball stroke play).

c *Playing Out of Turn*

If a competitor plays out of turn, no penalty is incurred and the ball shall be played as it lies. If, however, the Committee determines that competitors have agreed to play in an order other than that set forth in Clauses 2a and 2b of this Rule to give one of them an advantage, *they shall be disqualified.*

(Incorrect order of play in threesomes and foursomes stroke play— see Rule 29-3.)

Rule 10-3   Provisional Ball or Second Ball from Teeing Ground

If a player plays a **provisional ball** or a second ball from a **teeing ground**, he should do so after his opponent or fellow-competitor has played his first **stroke.** If a player plays a provisional ball or a second ball out of turn, Clauses 1c and 2c of this Rule shall apply.

Rule 10-4   Ball Moved in Measuring

If a ball is moved in measuring to determine which ball is farther from the hole, no penalty is incurred and the ball shall be replaced.

11

TEEING GROUND

The "teeing ground" is the starting place for the hole to be played. It is a rectangular area two club-lengths in depth, the front and the sides of which are defined by the outside limits of two tee-markers. A ball is outside the teeing ground when all of it lies outside the teeing ground.

Teeing — Rule 11-1

In teeing, the ball may be placed on the ground, on an irregularity of surface created by the player on the ground, or on a tee, sand or other substance in order to raise it off the ground.

A player may stand outside the **teeing ground** to play a ball within it.

Tee-Markers — Rule 11-2

Before a player plays his first stroke with any ball from the teeing ground of the hole being played, the tee-markers are deemed to be fixed. In such circumstances, if the player moves or allows to be moved a tee-marker for the purpose of avoiding interference with his stance, the area of his intended swing or his line of play, *he shall incur the penalty for a breach of Rule 13-2.*

Ball Falling Off Tee — Rule 11-3

If a ball, when not **in play**, falls off a tee or is knocked off a tee by the player in addressing it, it may be re-teed without penalty, but if a stroke is made at the ball in these circumstances, whether the ball is moving or not, the stroke counts but no penalty is incurred.

Playing from Outside Teeing Ground — Rule 11-4

a *Match Play*

If a player, when starting a hole, plays a ball from outside the **teeing ground**, the opponent may immediately require the player to cancel the stroke so played and play a ball from within the teeing ground, without penalty.

b *Stroke Play*

If a competitor, when starting a hole, plays a ball from outside the **teeing ground**, *he shall incur a penalty of two strokes* and shall then play a ball from within the teeing ground.

If the competitor plays a stroke from the next teeing ground without first correcting his mistake or, in the case of the last hole of the round, leaves the **putting green** without first declaring his intention to correct his mistake, *he shall be disqualified.*

Strokes played by a competitor from outside the teeing ground do not count in his score.

Playing from Wrong Teeing Ground — Rule 11-5

The provisions of Rule 11-4 apply.

12

SEARCHING FOR AND

IDENTIFYING BALL

Definitions

A "hazard" is any **bunker** *or* **water hazard**.

A "bunker" is a **hazard** *consisting of a prepared area of ground, often a hollow, from which turf or soil has been removed and replaced with sand or the like. Grass-covered ground bordering or within a bunker is not part of the bunker. The margin of a bunker extends vertically downwards, but not upwards.*

A "water hazard" is any sea, lake, pond, river, ditch, surface drainage ditch or other open water course (whether or not containing water) and anything of a similar nature.

All ground or water within the margin of a water hazard is part of the water hazard. The margin of a water hazard extends vertically upwards and downwards. Stakes and lines defining the margins of water hazards are in the hazards.

Rule 12-1   Searching for Ball; Seeing Ball

In searching for his ball anywhere on the course, the player may touch or bend long grass, rushes, bushes, whins, heather or the like, but only to the extent necessary to find and identify it, provided that this does not improve the lie of the ball, the area of his intended swing or his line of play.

A player is not necessarily entitled to see his ball when playing a stroke.

In a **hazard**, if a ball is covered by **loose impediments** or sand, the player may remove by probing, raking or other means as much thereof as will enable him to see a part of the ball. If an excess is removed, no penalty is incurred and the ball shall be re-covered so that only a part of the ball is visible. If the ball is moved in such removal, no penalty is incurred; the ball shall be replaced and, if necessary, re-covered. As to removal of loose impediments outside a hazard, see Rule 23.

If a ball lying in **casual water, ground under repair** or a hole, cast or runway made by a burrowing animal, a reptile or a bird is accidentally moved during search, no penalty is incurred; the ball shall be replaced, unless the player elects to proceed under Rule 25-1b.

If a ball is believed to be lying in water in a **water hazard**, the player may probe for it with a club or otherwise. If the ball is moved in so doing, no penalty is incurred; the ball shall be replaced, unless the player elects to proceed under Rule 26-1.

PENALTY FOR BREACH OF RULE 12-1: *Match play – Loss of hole; Stroke play – Two strokes.*

SEARCHING FOR BALL IN GROUND UNDER REPAIR

I've just moved my ball while searching for it. It's a good job it's in ground under repair because I can replace it where it lay, and play it without penalty, or I can take a free drop outside the G.U.R.

The responsibility for playing the proper ball rests with the player. Each player should put an identification mark on his ball.

Except in a **hazard**, the player may, without penalty, lift a ball he believes to be his own for the purpose of identification and clean it to the extent necessary for identification. If the ball is the player's ball, he shall replace it. Before lifting the ball, the player must announce his intention to his opponent in match play or his marker or a fellow-competitor in stroke play and mark the position of the ball. He must then give his opponent, marker or fellow-competitor an opportunity to observe the lifting and replacement. If he lifts his ball without announcing his intention in advance, marking the position of the ball or giving his opponent, marker or fellow-competitor an opportunity to observe, or if he lifts his ball for identification in a hazard, or cleans it more than necessary for identification *he shall incur a penalty of one stroke* and the ball shall be replaced.

If a player who is required to replace a ball fails to do so, *he shall incur the penalty* for a breach of Rule 20-3a, but no additional penalty under Rule 12-2 shall be applied.

I'm not sure if this is my ball; it's covered with mud and I can't identify it.

You will have to mark the position of the ball, lift it, and only remove enough mud to enable you to identify it. But don't lift it until I come over to watch.

13

BALL PLAYED AS IT LIES; LIE, AREA OF INTENDED SWING AND LINE OF PLAY; STANCE

Definitions

A "hazard" is any **bunker** *or* **water hazard***.*

A "bunker" is a **hazard** *consisting of a prepared area of ground, often a hollow, from which turf or soil has been removed and replaced with sand or the like. Grass-covered ground bordering or within a bunker is not part of the bunker. The margin of a bunker extends vertically downwards, but not upwards.*

A "water hazard" is any sea, lake, pond, river, ditch, surface drainage ditch or other open water course (whether or not containing water) and anything of a similar nature.

All ground or water within the margin of a water hazard is part of the water hazard. The margin of a water hazard extends vertically upwards and downwards. Stakes and lines defining the margins of water hazards are in the hazards.

The "line of play" is the direction which the player wishes his ball to take after a stroke, plus a reasonable distance on either side of the intended direction. The line of play extends vertically upwards from the ground, but does not extend beyond the hole.

Rule 13-1   Ball Played As It Lies

The ball shall be played as it lies, except as otherwise provided in the Rules. (Ball at rest moved – see Rule 18).

Rule 13-2   Improving Lie, Area of Intended Swing or Line of Play

Except as provided in the Rules, a player shall not improve or allow to be improved:

the position or lie of his ball,

the area of his intended swing,

his **line of play** or a reasonable extension of that line beyond the hole or

the area in which he is to drop or place a ball

by any of the following actions:

moving, bending or breaking anything growing or fixed (including immovable **obstructions** and objects defining **out of bounds**) or

removing or pressing down sand, loose soil, replaced divots, other cut turf placed in position or other irregularities of surface

except as follows:

as may occur in fairly taking his **stance**,

in making a **stroke** or the backward movement of his club for a stroke,

on the **teeing ground** in creating or eliminating irregularities of surface, or

on the **putting green** in removing sand and loose soil as provided in Rule 16-1a or in repairing damage as provided in Rule 16-1c.

IMPROVING AREA OF INTENDED SWING

A player must not move, bend or break anything growing or fixed.

Sand on the putting green is a loose impediment and may be removed. It is not permitted to move sand on the fringe or apron of the green.

BALL LYING IN BUNKER
Before making a stroke at a ball which lies in a bunker the player shall not

touch the ground with his club

smooth the sand or soil . . .

remove loose impediments . . .

touch a loose impediment with his club at address or on his backswing.

The club may be grounded only lightly and shall not be pressed on the ground.

Exception: Ball lying in or touching hazard — see Rule 13-4.

Building Stance — Rule 13-3

A player is entitled to place his feet firmly in taking his stance, but he shall not build a stance.

Ball Lying in or Touching Hazard — Rule 13-4

Except as provided in the Rules, before making a **stroke** at a ball which lies in or touches a **hazard** (whether a **bunker** or a **water hazard**), the player shall not:

a. Test the condition of the hazard or any similar hazard,

b. Touch the ground in the hazard or water in the water hazard with a club or otherwise, or

c. Touch or move a **loose impediment** lying in or touching the hazard.

Exceptions:

1. Provided nothing is done which constitutes testing the condition of the hazard or improves the lie of the ball, there is no penalty if the player (a) touches the ground in any hazard or water in a water hazard as a result of or to prevent falling, in removing an **obstruction**, in measuring or in retrieving or lifting a ball under any Rule or (b) places his clubs in a hazard.

2. The player after playing the stroke, or his **caddie** at any time without the authority of the player, may smooth sand or soil in the hazard, provided that, if the ball still lies in the hazard, nothing is done which improves the lie of the ball or assists the player in his subsequent play of the hole.

Note: At any time, including at address or in the backward movement for the stroke, the player may touch with a club or otherwise any obstruction, any construction declared by the Committee to be an integral part of the course or any grass, bush, tree or other growing thing.

PENALTY FOR BREACH OF RULE: *Match play — Loss of hole; Stroke play — Two strokes.*

(Searching for ball — see Rule 12-1.)

STRIKING THE BALL

14

Definition

A "stroke" is the forward movement of the club made with the intention of fairly striking at and moving the ball, but if a player checks his downswing voluntarily before the clubhead reaches the ball he is deemed not to have made a stroke.

Ball to be Fairly Struck At — Rule 14-1

The ball shall be fairly struck at with the head of the club and must not be pushed, scraped or spooned.

Rule 14-2　　　Assistance

In making a **stroke**, a player shall not accept physical assistance or protection from the elements.

PENALTY FOR BREACH OF RULE 14-1 or -2: *Match play — Loss of hole; Stroke play — Two strokes.*

Rule 14-3　　　Artificial Devices and Unusual Equipment

If there may be any reasonable basis for doubt as to whether an item which is to be manufactured would, if used by a player during a round, cause the player to be in breach of Rule 14-3, the manufacturer should submit a sample to the Royal and Ancient Golf Club of St. Andrews for a ruling, such sample to become its property for reference purposes. If a manufacturer fails to do so, he assumes the risk of an unfavourable ruling.

A player in doubt as to whether use of an item would constitute a breach of Rule 14-3 should consult the Royal and Ancient Golf Club of St. Andrews.

Except as provided in the Rules, during a **stipulated round** the player shall not use any artificial device or unusual equipment:

a. Which might assist him in making a stroke or in his play; or

b. For the purpose of gauging or measuring distance or conditions which might affect his play; or

c. Which might assist him in gripping the club, except that plain gloves may be worn, resin, tape or gauze may be applied to the grip (provided such application does not render the grip non-conforming under Rule 4-1c) and a towel or handkerchief may be wrapped around the grip.

PENALTY FOR BREACH OF RULE 14-3: *Disqualification.*

Striking the Ball More than Once — Rule 14-4

If a player's club strikes the ball more than once in the course of a **stroke**, the player shall count the stroke and *add a penalty stroke,* making two strokes in all.

Playing Moving Ball — Rule 14-5

A player shall not play while his ball is moving.
Exceptions:
Ball falling off tee – Rule 11-3.
Striking the ball more than once – Rule 14-4.
Ball moving in water – Rule 14-6.
When the ball begins to move only after the player has begun the **stroke** or the backward movement of his club for the stroke, he shall incur no penalty under this Rule for playing a moving ball, but he is not exempt from any penalty incurred under the following Rules:
Ball at rest moved by player – Rule 18-2a.
Ball at rest moving after address – Rule 18-2b.
Ball at rest moving after loose impediment touched – Rule 18-2c.

Ball Moving in Water — Rule 14-6

When a ball is moving in water in a **water hazard**, the player may, without penalty, make a **stroke**, but he must not delay making his stroke in order to allow the wind or current to improve the position of the ball. A ball moving in water in a water hazard may be lifted if the player elects to invoke Rule 26.
PENALTY FOR BREACH OF RULE 14-5 or -6: *Match play – Loss of hole; Stroke play – Two strokes.*

PLAYING A WRONG BALL

A "wrong ball" is any ball other than: **Definition**
a. The **ball in play**,
b. A **provisional ball** *or*
c. In stroke play, a second ball played under Rule 3-3 or Rule 20-7b.
Note: Ball in play includes a ball substituted for the ball in play when the player is proceeding under an applicable Rule which does not permit substitution.

General — Rule 15-1

A player must hole out with the ball played from the **teeing ground** unless a Rule permits him to substitute another ball. If a player substitutes another ball when proceeding under an applicable Rule which does not permit substitution, that ball is not a **wrong ball**; it becomes the **ball in play** and, if the error is not corrected as provided in Rule 20-6, *the player shall incur a penalty of loss of hole in match play or two strokes in stroke play.*

43

PLAYING A SUBSTITUTED BALL

Match Play   Rule 15-2

If a player plays a stroke with a **wrong ball** except in a **hazard**, *he shall lose the hole.*

If a player plays any strokes in a hazard with a wrong ball, there is no penalty. Strokes played in a hazard with a wrong ball do not count in the player's score. If the wrong ball belongs to another player, its owner shall place a ball on the spot from which the wrong ball was first played.

If the player and opponent exchange balls during the play of a hole, the first to play the wrong ball other than from a hazard shall lose the hole; when this cannot be determined, the hole shall be played out with the balls exchanged.

Rule 15-3   Stroke Play

If a competitor plays a stroke or strokes with a **wrong ball**, *he shall incur a penalty of two strokes,* unless the only stroke or strokes played with such ball were played when it was lying in a hazard, in which case no penalty is incurred.

The competitor must correct his mistake by playing the correct ball. If he fails to correct his mistake before he plays a stroke from the next **teeing ground** or, in the case of the last hole of the round, fails to declare his intention to correct his mistake before leaving the **putting green**, *he shall be disqualified.*

Strokes played by a competitor with a wrong ball do not count in his score.

If the wrong ball belongs to another competitor, its owner shall place a ball on the spot from which the wrong ball was first played.

(Lie of ball to be placed or replaced altered — see Rule 20-3b.)

16

THE PUTTING GREEN

The "putting green" is all ground of the hole being played which is specially prepared for putting or otherwise defined as such by the Committee. A ball is on the putting green when any part of it touches the putting green.

The "line of putt" is the line which the player wishes his ball to take after a stroke on the **putting green**. Except with respect to Rule 16-1e, the line of putt includes a reasonable distance on either side of the intended line. The line of putt does not extend beyond the hole.

A ball is "holed" when it is at rest within the circumference of the hole and all of it is below the level of the lip of the hole.

a *Touching Line of Putt*

The **line of putt** must not be touched except:

(i)   the player may move sand and loose soil on the putting green and other **loose impediments** by picking them up or by brushing them aside with his hand or a club without pressing anything down;

(ii)   in addressing the ball, the player may place the club in front of the ball without pressing anything down;

(iii)   in measuring – Rule 10-4;

(iv)   in lifting the ball – Rule 16-lb;

(v)   in pressing down a ball-marker;

(vi)   in repairing old hole plugs or ball marks on the putting green – Rule 16-lc; and

(vii)   in removing movable **obstructions** – Rule 24-1.

(Indicating line for putting on putting green – see Rule 8-2b.)

TOUCHING LINE OF PUTT

a
b
c
d

Examples of when the line of putt may be touched without penalty: (**a**) placing the clubhead in front of the ball without pressing anything down when addressing the ball;(**b**) removing a loose impediment, such as a leaf or a twig;(**c**) repairing a ball mark; (**d**) repairing an old hole plug.

b *Lifting Ball*   A ball on the **putting green** may be lifted and, if desired, cleaned. A ball so lifted shall be replaced on the spot from which it was lifted.

c *Repair of Hole Plugs, Ball Marks and Other Damage*   The player may repair an old hole plug or damage to the **putting green** caused by the impact of a ball, whether or not the player's ball lies on the putting green. If the ball is moved in the process of such repair, it shall be replaced, without penalty. Any other damage to the putting green shall not be repaired if it might assist the player in his subsequent play of the hole.

d *Testing Surface*   During the play of a hole, a player shall not test the surface of the **putting green** by rolling a ball or roughening or scraping the surface.

e *Standing Astride or On Line of Putt*   The player shall not make a **stroke** on the **putting green** from a **stance** astride, or with either foot touching, the line of putt or an extension of that line behind the ball.

f *Position of Caddie or Partner*   While making a stroke on the putting green, the player shall not allow his caddie, his partner or his partner's caddie to position himself on or close to an extension of the line of putt behind the ball.

g *Playing Stroke While Another Ball in Motion*   The player shall not play a stroke while another ball is in motion after a stroke from the putting green, except that, if a player does so, he incurs no penalty if it was his turn to play.

(Lifting ball interfering with or assisting play while another ball in motion — see Rule 22.)

PENALTY FOR BREACH OF RULE 16-1: *Match play — Loss of hole; Stroke play — Two strokes.*

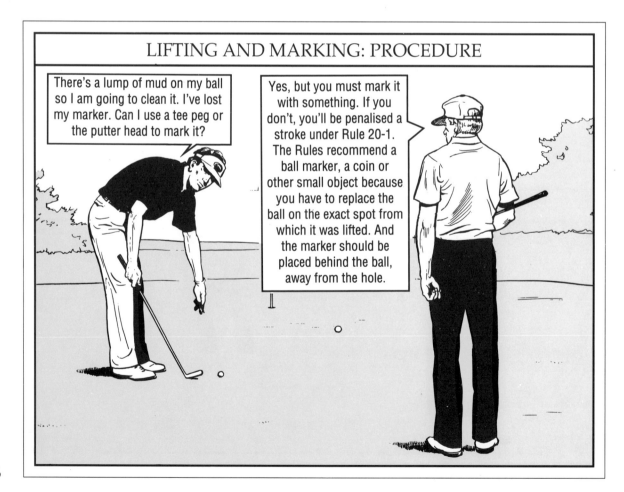

LIFTING AND MARKING: PROCEDURE

There's a lump of mud on my ball so I am going to clean it. I've lost my marker. Can I use a tee peg or the putter head to mark it?

Yes, but you must mark it with something. If you don't, you'll be penalised a stroke under Rule 20-1. The Rules recommend a ball marker, a coin or other small object because you have to replace the ball on the exact spot from which it was lifted. And the marker should be placed behind the ball, away from the hole.

Rule 16-2 Ball Overhanging Hole

When any part of the ball overhangs the lip of the hole, the player is allowed enough time to reach the hole without unreasonable delay and an additional ten seconds to determine whether the ball is at rest. If by then the ball has not fallen into the hole, it is deemed to be at rest. If the ball subsequently falls into the hole, the player is deemed to have holed out with his last stroke, and *he shall add a penalty stroke to his score* for the hole; otherwise there is no penalty under this Rule.

(Undue delay — see Rule 6-7.).

17

THE FLAGSTICK

Rule 17-1   Flagstick Attended, Removed or Held Up

Before and during the **stroke**, the player may have the flagstick attended, removed or held up to indicate the position of the hole. This may be done only on the authority of the player before he plays his stroke.

    If, prior to the stroke, the flagstick is attended, removed or held up by anyone with the player's knowledge and no objection is made, the player shall be deemed to have authorised it. If anyone attends or holds up the flagstick or stands near the hole while a stroke is being played, he shall be deemed to be attending the flagstick until the ball comes to rest.

Rule 17-2   Unauthorised Attendance

a *Match Play*

In match play, an opponent or his caddie shall not, without the authority or prior knowledge of the player, attend, remove or hold up the flagstick while the player is making a stroke or his ball is in motion.

FLAGSTICK ATTENDED BY PLAYER HIMSELF

It is permissible to hold the flagstick with one hand and to putt with the other provided the flagstick has been removed and the ball therefore does not strike it.

ADJUSTMENT OF THE FLAGSTICK – PLAYER'S BALL OFF THE GREEN

FLAGSTICK HELD UP TO INDICATE POSITION OF HOLE

b *Stroke Play* In stroke play, if a fellow-competitor or his caddie attends, removes or holds up the flagstick without the competitor's authority or prior knowledge while the competitor is making a stroke or his ball is in motion, *the fellow-competitor shall incur the penalty* for breach of this Rule. In such circumstances, if the competitor's ball strikes the flagstick, the person attending it or anything carried by him, the competitor incurs no penalty and the ball shall be played as it lies, except that, if the stroke was played from the putting green, the stroke shall be cancelled, the ball replaced and the stroke replayed.

PENALTY FOR BREACH OF RULE 17-1 or -2: *Match play – Loss of hole; Stroke play – Two Strokes.*

Rule 17-3   Ball Striking Flagstick or Attendant

The player's ball shall not strike:

a. The flagstick when attended, removed or held up by the player, his partner or either of their caddies, or by another person with the player's authority or prior knowledge; or

b. The player's caddie, his partner or his partner's caddie when attending the flagstick, or another person attending the flagstick with the player's authority or prior knowledge, or anything carried by any such person; or

c. The flagstick in the hole, unattended, when the ball has been played from the **putting green**.

PENALTY FOR BREACH OF RULE 17-3: *Match play – Loss of hole; Stroke play – Two strokes, and the ball shall be played as it lies.*

Rule 17-4   Ball Resting Against Flagstick

If the ball rests against the flagstick when it is in the hole, the player or another person authorised by him may move or remove the flagstick and if the ball falls into the hole, the player shall be deemed to have holed out with his last stroke; otherwise the ball, if **moved**, shall be placed on the lip of the hole, without penalty.

BALL AT REST MOVED

18

Definitions

A ball is deemed to have "moved" if it leaves its position and comes to rest in any other place.

An "outside agency" is any agency not part of the match or, in stroke play, not part of the competitor's side, and includes a referee, a marker, an observer or a forecaddie. Neither wind nor water is an outside agency.

"Equipment" is anything used, worn or carried by or for the player except any ball he has played at the hole being played and any small object, such as a coin or a tee, when used to mark the position of a ball or the extent of an area in which a ball is to be dropped. Equipment includes a golf cart, whether or not motorised. If such a cart is shared by two or more players, the cart and everything in it are deemed to be the equipment of the player whose ball is involved except that, when the cart is being moved by one of the players sharing it, the cart and everything in it are deemed to be that player's equipment.

*Note: A ball played at the hole being played is equipment when it has been lifted and not put back into play. A player has "addressed the ball" when he has taken his **stance** and has also grounded his club, except that in a **hazard** a player has addressed the ball when he has taken his stance.*

*Taking the "stance" consists in a player placing his feet in position for and preparatory to making a **stroke**.*

By Outside Agency   Rule 18-1

If a ball at rest is moved by an **outside agency**, the player shall incur no penalty and the ball shall be replaced before the player plays another **stroke**.

(Player's ball at rest moved by another ball – see Rule 18-5.)

By Player, Partner, Caddie or Equipment   Rule 18-2

When a player's ball is **in play**, if:

a *General*

(i) the player, his partner or either of their caddies lifts or moves it, touches it purposely (except with a club in the act of addressing it) or causes it to move except as permitted by a Rule, or

(ii) equipment of the player or his partner causes the ball to move,

the player shall incur a penalty stroke. The ball shall be replaced unless the movement of the ball occurs after the player has begun his swing and he does not discontinue his swing.

Under the Rules no penalty is incurred if a player accidentally causes his ball to move in the following circumstances:

In measuring to determine which ball farther from hole – Rule 10-4

In searching for covered ball in **hazard** or for ball in **casual water**, **ground under repair**, etc. – Rule 12-1

In the process of repairing hole plug or ball mark – Rule 16-1c

In the process of removing **loose impediments** on **putting green** – Rule 18-2c

In the process of lifting ball under a Rule – Rule 20-1.

In the process of placing or replacing ball under a Rule – Rule 20-3a

In complying with Rule 22 relating to lifting ball interfering with or assisting play

In removal of movable **obstruction** – Rule 24-1

b *Ball Moving After Address*

If a player's **ball in play moves** after he has **addressed** it (other than as a result of a stroke), the player shall be deemed to have moved the ball and *shall incur a penalty stroke.* The player shall replace the ball unless the movement of the ball occurs after he has begun his swing and he does not discontinue his swing.

c *Ball Moving After Loose Impediment Touched*

Through the green, if the ball **moves** after any **loose impediment** lying within a club-length of it has been touched by the player, his partner or either of their caddies and before the player has **addressed** it, the player shall be deemed to have moved the ball and *shall incur a penalty stroke.* The player shall replace the ball unless the movement of the ball occurs after he has begun his swing and he does not discontinue his swing.

On the **putting green**, if the ball or the ball-marker **moves** in the process of removing any **loose impediment**, the ball or the ball-marker shall be replaced. There is no penalty provided the movement of the ball or the ball-marker is directly attributable to the removal of the loose impediment. Otherwise, *the player shall incur a penalty stroke* under Rule 18-2a or 20-1.

By Opponent, Caddie or Equipment in Match Play   Rule 18-3

If, during search for a player's ball, it is moved by an opponent, his caddie or his **equipment**, no penalty is incurred and the player shall replace the ball.

a *During Search*

If, other than during search for a ball, the ball is touched or moved by an opponent, his caddie or his **equipment**, except as otherwise provided in the Rules, *the opponent shall incur a penalty stroke*. The player shall replace the ball.

b *Other Than During Search*

    (Ball moved in measuring to determine which ball farther from the hole – see Rule 10-4.)

    (Playing a wrong ball – see Rule 15-2.)

    (Ball moved in complying with Rule 22 relating to lifting ball interfering with or assisting play.)

By Fellow-Competitor, Caddie or Equipment in Stroke Play   Rule 18-4

If a competitor's ball is moved by a fellow-competitor, his caddie or his **equipment**, no penalty is incurred. The competitor shall replace his ball.

    (Playing a wrong ball – see Rule 15-3.)

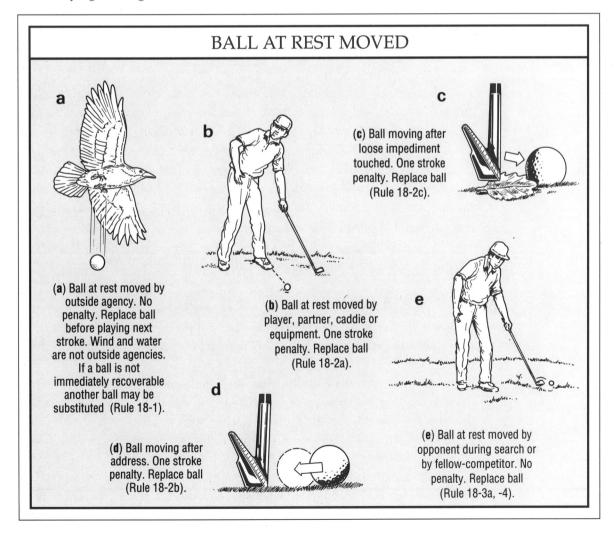

BALL AT REST MOVED

(a) Ball at rest moved by outside agency. No penalty. Replace ball before playing next stroke. Wind and water are not outside agencies. If a ball is not immediately recoverable another ball may be substituted (Rule 18-1).

(b) Ball at rest moved by player, partner, caddie or equipment. One stroke penalty. Replace ball (Rule 18-2a).

(c) Ball moving after loose impediment touched. One stroke penalty. Replace ball (Rule 18-2c).

(d) Ball moving after address. One stroke penalty. Replace ball (Rule 18-2b).

(e) Ball at rest moved by opponent during search or by fellow-competitor. No penalty. Replace ball (Rule 18-3a, -4).

If a ball in play and at rest is moved by another ball in motion after a stroke, the moved ball shall be replaced.

PENALTY FOR BREACH OF RULE: *Match play – Loss of hole; Stroke play – Two strokes. If a player who is required to replace a ball fails to do so, he shall incur the general penalty for breach of Rule 18 but no additional penalty under Rule 18 shall be applied.*

Note 1: If a ball to be replaced under this Rule is not immediately recoverable, another ball may be substituted

Note 2: If it is impossible to determine the spot on which a ball is to be placed, see Rule 20-3c.

19

BALL IN MOTION DEFLECTED

OR STOPPED

Definitions

An "outside agency" is any agency not part of the match or, in stroke play, not part of the competitor's side, and includes a referee, a marker, an observer or a forecaddie. Neither wind nor water is an outside agency.

"Equipment" is anything used, worn or carried by or for the player except any ball he has played at the hole being played and any small object, such as a coin or a tee, when used to mark the position of a ball or the extent of an area in which a ball is to be dropped. Equipment includes a golf cart, whether or not motorised. If such a cart is shared by two or more players, the cart and everything in it are deemed to be the equipment of the player whose ball is involved except that, when the cart is being moved by one of the players sharing it, the cart and everything in it are deemed to be that player's equipment.

Note: A ball played at the hole being played is equipment when it has been lifted and not put back into play.

If a ball in motion is accidentally deflected or stopped by any **outside agency**, it is a **rub of the green**, no penalty is incurred and the ball shall be played as it lies except:

a. If a ball in motion after a **stroke** other than on the **putting green** comes to rest in or on any moving or animate outside agency, the player shall, **through the green** or in a **hazard**, drop the ball, or on the putting green place the ball, as near as possible to the spot where the outside agency was when the ball came to rest in or on it, and

b. If a ball in motion after a stroke on the putting green is deflected or stopped by, or comes to rest in or on, any moving or animate outside agency except a worm or an insect, the stroke shall be cancelled, the ball replaced and the stroke replayed.

If the ball is not immediately recoverable, another ball may be substituted.

(Player's ball deflected or stopped by another ball — see Rule 19-5.)

Note: If the referee or the Committee determines that a player's ball has been purposely deflected or stopped by an **outside agency**, Rule 1-4 applies to the player. If the outside agency is a fellow-competitor or his caddie, Rule 1-2 applies to the fellow-competitor.

By Player, Partner, Caddie or Equipment   Rule 19-2

If a player's ball is accidentally deflected or stopped by himself, his partner or either of their caddies or **equipment**, *he shall lose the hole.*   **a** *Match Play*

If a competitor's ball is accidentally deflected or stopped by himself, his partner or either of their caddies or **equipment**, *the competitor shall incur a penalty of two strokes.* The ball shall be played as it lies, except when it comes to rest in or on the competitor's, his partner's or either of their caddies' clothes or equipment, in which case the competitor shall **through the green** or in a **hazard** drop the ball, or on the **putting green** place the ball, as near as possible to where the article was when the ball came to rest in or on it.   **b** *Stroke Play*

Exception: Dropped Ball – see Rule 20-2a.

(Ball purposely deflected or stopped by player, partner or caddie – see Rule 1-2.)

BALL IN MOTION DEFLECTED OR STOPPED

1 Outside agency
No penalty

2 Match play
Player's own caddie
Player loses hole

3 Match play
Opponent's caddie,
accidentally
*No penalty. Player has
option to replay*

4 Stroke play
Player's own caddie
Two-stroke penalty

5 Stroke play
Fellow-competitor's
caddie
*No penalty, but see
Note to Rule 19-1
for exception.*

Rule 19-3　　By Opponent, Caddie or Equipment in Match Play

If a player's ball is accidentally deflected or stopped by an opponent, his caddie or his **equipment**, no penalty is incurred. The player may play the ball as it lies or, before another **stroke** is played by either side, cancel the stroke and play a ball without penalty as nearly as posible at the spot from which the original ball was last played (see Rule 20-5).

If the ball has come to rest in or on the opponent's or his caddie's clothes or equipment, the player may **through the green** or in a **hazard** drop the ball, or on the putting green place the ball, as near as possible to where the article was when the ball came to rest in or on it.

Exception: Ball striking person attending flagstick – see Rule 17-3b.

(Ball purposely deflected or stopped by opponent or caddie – see Rule 1-2.)

Rule 19-4　　By Fellow-Competitor, Caddie or Equipment in Stroke Play

See Rule 19-1 regarding ball deflected by outside agency.

Rule 19-5　　By Another Ball

If a player's ball in motion after a stroke is deflected or stopped by a ball at rest, the player shall play his ball as it lies. In stroke play, if both balls lay on the **putting green** prior to the stroke, *the player incurs a penalty of two strokes*. Otherwise, no penalty is incurred.

If a player's ball in motion after a stroke is deflected or stopped by another ball in motion, the player shall play his ball as it lies. There is no penalty unless the player was in breach of Rule 16-1g, in which case *he shall incur the penalty for breach of that Rule.*

Exception: Ball in motion after a stroke on the putting green deflected or stopped by moving or animate outside agency – see Rule 19-1b.

PENALTY FOR BREACH OF RULE: *Match play – Loss of hole; Stroke play – Two strokes.*

LIFTING, DROPPING AND PLACING;

PLAYING FROM WRONG PLACE

20

Lifting   **Rule 20-1**

A ball to be lifted under the Rules may be lifted by the player, his partner or another person authorised by the player. In any such case, the player shall be responsible for any breach of the Rules.

The position of the ball shall be marked before it is lifted under a Rule which requires it to be replaced. If it is not marked, *the player shall incur a penalty of one stroke* and the ball shall be replaced. If it is not replaced, *the player shall incur the general penalty* for breach of this Rule but no additional penalty under Rule 20-1 shall be applied.

If a ball or the ball-marker is accidentally moved in the process of lifting the ball under a Rule or marking its position, the ball or the ball-marker shall be replaced. There is no penalty provided the movement of the ball or the ball-marker is directly attributable to the specific act of marking the position of or lifting the ball. Otherwise, *the player shall incur a penalty stroke* under this Rule or Rule 18-2a. *Exception*: If a player incurs a penalty for failing to act in accordance with Rule 5-3 or 12-2, no additional penalty under Rule 20-1 shall be applied.

Note: The position of a ball to be lifted should be marked by placing a ball-marker, a small coin or other similar object immediately behind the ball. If the ball-marker interferes with the play, **stance** or **stroke** of another player, it should be placed one or more clubhead-lengths to one side.

Rule 20-2   Dropping and Re-dropping

a *By Whom and How*

A ball to be dropped under the Rules shall be dropped by the player himself. He shall stand erect, hold the ball at shoulder height and arm's length and drop it. If a ball is dropped by any other person or in any other manner and the error is not corrected as provided in Rule 20-6, *the player shall incur a penalty stroke.*

If the ball touches the player, his partner, either of their caddies or their equipment before or after it strikes a part of the course, the ball shall be re-dropped, without penalty. There is no limit to the number of times a ball shall be re-dropped in such circumstances.

(Taking action to influence position or movement of ball — see Rule 1-2.)

DROPPING BALL: HOW TO DROP

A ball to be dropped under the Rules shall be dropped by the player himself. He shall stand erect, hold the ball at shoulder height and arm's length and drop it.

b *Where to Drop*

When a ball is to be dropped as near as possible to a specific spot, it shall be dropped not nearer the hole than the specific spot which, if it is not precisely known to the player, shall be estimated.

A ball when dropped must first strike a part of the course where the applicable Rule requires it to be dropped. If it is not so dropped, Rules 20-6 and -7 apply.

c *When to Re-Drop*

A dropped ball shall be re-dropped without penalty if it:
(i)   rolls into a **hazard**;
(ii)   rolls out of a hazard;
(iii) rolls onto a **putting green**;
(iv)   rolls **out of bounds**;
(v)   rolls to a position where there is interference by the condition from which relief was taken under Rule 24-2 (immovable obstruction) or Rule 25-1 (abnormal ground condition);
(vi)   rolls and comes to rest more than two club-lengths from where it first struck a part of the course; or
(vii) rolls and comes to rest nearer the hole than its original position or estimated position (see Rule 20-2b) unless otherwise permitted by the Rules.
If the ball when re-dropped rolls into any position listed above, it shall be placed as near as possible to the spot where it first struck a part of the course when re-dropped.

If a ball to be re-dropped or placed under this Rule is not immediately recoverable, another ball may be substituted.

> A dropped ball must be redropped without penalty if it rolls:
> (**i**) into a hazard;
> (**ii**) out of a hazard;
> (**iii**) onto a putting green;
> (**iv**) out of bounds;
> (**v**) back into condition;
> (**vi**) more than 2 club-lengths;
> (**vii**) nearer the hole than its original position.

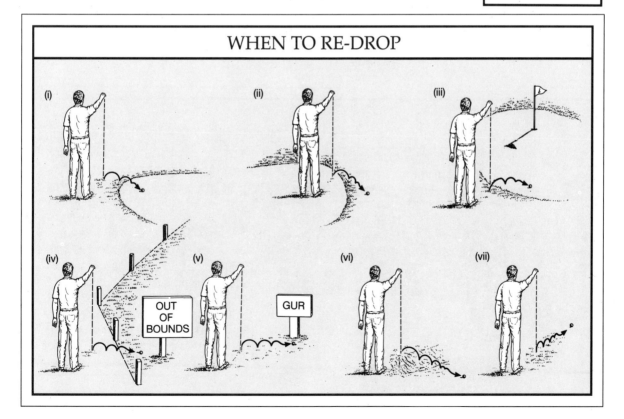

WHEN TO RE-DROP

Rule 20-3   Placing and Replacing

a *By Whom and Where*

A ball to be placed under the Rules shall be placed by the player or his partner. If a ball is to be replaced, the player, his partner or the person who lifted or moved it shall place it on the spot from which it was lifted or moved. In any such case, the player shall be responsible for any breach of the Rules.

If a ball or the ball-marker is accidentally moved in the process of placing or replacing the ball, the ball or the ball-marker shall be replaced. There is no penalty provided the movement of the ball or the ball-marker is directly attributable to the specific act of placing or replacing the ball or removing the ball-marker. Otherwise, *the player shall incur a penalty stroke* under Rule 18-2a or 20-1.

b *Lie of Ball to be Placed or Replaced Altered*

If the original lie of a ball to be placed or replaced has been altered:

(i)   except in a **hazard**, the ball shall be placed in the nearest lie most similar to the original lie which is not more than one club-length from the original lie, not nearer the hole and not in a hazard;

(ii)   in a **water hazard**, the ball shall be placed in accordance with Clause (i) above, except that the ball must be placed in the water hazard;

(iii)   In a **bunker**, the original lie shall be recreated as nearly as possible and the ball shall be placed in that lie.

If it is impossible to determine the spot where the ball is to be placed or replaced:

c *Spot Not Determinable*

(i)   **through the green**, the ball shall be dropped as near as possible to the place where it lay but not in a **hazard**;

(ii)   In a hazard, the ball shall be dropped in the hazard as near as possible to the place where it lay;

(iii)   on the **putting green**, the ball shall be placed as near as possible to the place where it lay but not in a hazard.

If a ball when placed fails to remain on the spot on which it was placed, it shall be replaced without penalty. If it still fails to remain on that spot:

(i)   except in a **hazard,** it shall be placed at the nearest spot not nearer the hole or in a hazard where it can be placed at rest;

(ii) in a hazard, it shall be placed in the hazard at the nearest spot not nearer the hole where it can be placed at rest.

d *Ball Fails to Remain on Spot*

PENALTY FOR BREACH OF RULE 20-1, -2 or -3: *Match play – Loss of hole; Stroke play – Two strokes.*

When Ball Dropped or Placed Is in Play   Rule 20-4

If the player's **ball in play** has been lifted, it is again in play when dropped or placed.

A substituted ball becomes the ball in play if it is dropped or placed under an applicable Rule, whether or not such Rule permits substitution. A ball substituted under an inapplicable Rule is a **wrong ball**.

Playing Next Stroke from Where Previous Stroke Played   Rule 20-5

When, under the Rules, a player elects or is required to play his next **stroke** from where a previous stroke was played, he shall proceed as follows: if the stroke is to be played from the **teeing ground**, the ball to be played shall be played from anywhere within the teeing ground and may be teed; if the stroke is to be played from **through the green** or a **hazard**, it shall be dropped; if the stroke is to be played on the **putting green**, it shall be placed.

PENALTY FOR BREACH OF RULE 20-5: *Match play – Loss of hole; Stroke play – Two strokes.*

Lifting Ball Wrongly Dropped or Placed   Rule 20-6

A ball dropped or placed in a wrong place or otherwise not in accordance with the Rules but not played may be lifted, without penalty, and the player shall then proceed correctly.

61

Rule 20-7   Playing from Wrong Place

For a ball played from outside the teeing ground or from a wrong teeing ground – see Rule 11-4 and -5.

a *Match Play*

If a player plays a stroke with a ball which has been dropped or placed in a wrong place, *he shall lose the hole.*

b *Stroke Play*

If a competitor plays a stroke with (i) his original ball which has been dropped or placed in a wrong place, (ii) a substituted ball which has been dropped or placed under an applicable Rule but in a wrong place or (iii) his ball in play when it has been moved and not replaced in a case where the Rules require replacement, *he shall*, provided a serious breach has not occurred, *incur the penalty prescribed by the applicable Rule* and play out the hole with the ball.

If, after playing from a wrong place, a competitor becomes aware of that fact and believes that a serious breach may be involved, he may, provided he has not played a stroke from the next teeing ground or, in the case of the last hole of the round, left the putting green, declare that he will play out the hole with a second ball dropped or placed in accordance with the Rules. The competitor shall report the facts to the Committee before returning his score card; if he fails to do so, *he shall be disqualified.* The Committee shall determine whether a serious breach of the Rule occurred. If so, the score with the second ball shall count and *the competitor shall add two penalty strokes to his score with that ball.*

If a serious breach has occurred and the competitor has failed to correct it as prescribed above, *he shall be disqualifed.*

Note: If a competitor plays a second ball, penalty strokes incurred by playing the ball ruled not to count and strokes subsequently taken with that ball shall be disregarded.

21

CLEANING BALL

A ball on the putting green may be cleaned when lifted under Rule 16-1b. Elsewhere, a ball may be cleaned when lifted except when it has been lifted:
a. To determine if it is unfit for play (Rule 5-3);
b. For identification (Rule 12-2), in which case it may be cleaned only to the extent necessary for identification; or
c. Because it is interfering with or assisting play (Rule 22).

If a player cleans his ball during play of a hole except as provided in this Rule, *he shall incur a penalty of one stroke* and the ball, if lifted, shall be replaced.

If a player who is required to replace a ball fails to do so, *he shall incur the penalty* for breach of Rule 20-3a, but no additional penalty under Rule 21 shall be applied.

Exception: If a player incurs a penalty for failing to act in accordance with Rule 5-3, 12-2 or 22, no additional penalty under Rule 21 shall be applied.

22

BALL INTERFERING WITH

OR ASSISTING PLAY

Any player may:

    a. Lift his ball if he considers that the ball might assist any other player or

    b. Have any other ball lifted if he considers that the ball might interfere with his play or assist the play of any other player,

but this may not be done while another ball is in motion. In stroke play, a player required to lift his ball may play first rather than lift. A ball lifted under this Rule shall be replaced.

    If a ball is accidentally moved in complying with this Rule, no penalty is incurred and the ball shall be replaced.

PENALTY FOR BREACH OF RULE: *Match play – Loss of hole; Stroke play – Two strokes.*

Note: Except on the putting green, the ball may not be cleaned when lifted under this Rule – see Rule 21.

23

LOOSE IMPEDIMENTS

Definition

"Loose impediments" are natural objects such as stones, leaves, twigs, branches and the like, dung, worms and insects and casts or heaps made by them, provided they are not fixed or growing, are not solidly embedded and do not adhere to the ball.

    Sand and loose soil are loose impediments on the **putting green** *but not elsewhere.*

    Snow and natural ice, other than frost, are either **casual water** *or loose impediments, at the option of the player. Manufactured ice is an* **obstruction***.*

    Dew and frost are not loose impediments.

Rule 23-1 Relief

Except when both the **loose impediment** and the ball lie in or touch a **hazard**, any loose impediment may be removed without penalty. If the ball moves, see Rule 18-2c.

When a player's ball is in motion, a loose impediment which might influence the movement of the ball shall not be removed.

PENALTY FOR BREACH OF RULE: *Match play – Loss of hole; Stroke play – Two strokes.*

(Searching for ball in hazard — see Rule 12-1.)

(Touching line of putt — see Rule 16-1a.)

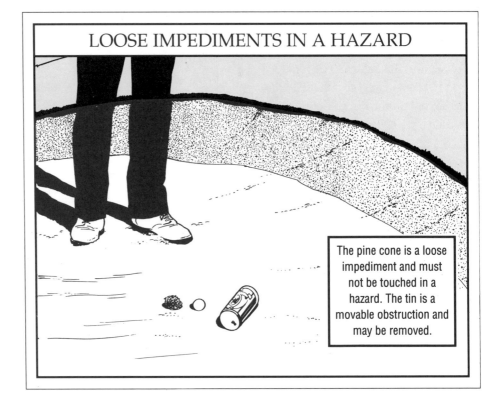

LOOSE IMPEDIMENTS IN A HAZARD

The pine cone is a loose impediment and must not be touched in a hazard. The tin is a movable obstruction and may be removed.

24

OBSTRUCTIONS

Definition

An "obstruction" is anything artificial, including the artificial surfaces and sides of roads and paths and manufactured ice, except:

*a. Objects defining **out of bounds**, such as walls, fences, stakes and railings;*

b. Any part of an immovable artificial object which is out of bounds; and

c. Any construction declared by the Committee to be an integral part of the course.

Movable Obstruction Rule 24-1

A player may obtain relief from a movable **obstruction** as follows:

a. If the ball does not lie in or on the obstruction, the obstruction may be removed. If the ball moves, it shall be replaced, and there is no penalty provided that the movement of the ball is directly attributable to the removal of the obstruction. Otherwise, Rule 18-2a applies.

b. If the ball lies in or on the obstruction, the ball may be lifted, without penalty, and the obstruction removed. The ball shall **through the green** or in a **hazard** be dropped, or on the **putting green** be placed, as near as possible to the spot directly under the place where the ball lay in or on the obstruction, but not nearer the hole.

The ball may be cleaned when lifted under Rule 24-1.

When a ball is in motion, an obstruction which might influence the movement of the ball, other than an attended flagstick or equipment of the players, shall not be removed.

Immovable Obstruction Rule 24-2

a *Interference*

Interference by an immovable **obstruction** occurs when a ball lies in or on the obstruction, or so close to the obstruction that the obstruction interferes with the player's **stance** or the area of his intended swing. If the player's ball lies on the **putting green**, interference also occurs if an immovable obstruction on the putting green intervenes on his line of putt. Otherwise, intervention on the line of play is not, of itself, interference under this Rule.

65

ROADS AND PATHS

Am I entitled to relief without penalty from this road?

Yes. The road is an immovable obstruction, but your nearest point of relief will be in the bushes. You can, of course, play it as it lies.

b *Relief*

Except when the ball lies in or touches a **water hazard** or a **lateral water hazard**, a player may obtain relief from interference by an immovable **obstruction**, without penalty, as follows:

(i) **Through the Green:** if the ball lies **through the green**, the point on the **course** nearest to where the ball lies shall be determined (without crossing over, through or under the obstruction) which (a) is not nearer the hole, (b) avoids interference (as defined) and (c) is not in a **hazard** or on a **putting green**. The player shall lift the ball and drop it within one club-length of the point thus determined on ground which fulfils (a), (b) and (c) above.

Note: The prohibition against crossing over, through or under the **obstruction** does not apply to the artificial surfaces and sides of roads and paths or when the ball lies in or on the obstruction.

(ii) **In a Bunker:** If the ball lies in or touches a **bunker**, the player shall lift and drop the ball in accordance with Clause (i) above, except that the ball must be dropped in the bunker.

(iii) **On the Putting Green:** If the ball lies on the **putting green**, the player shall lift the ball and place it in the nearest position to where it lay which affords relief from interference, but not nearer the hole nor in a hazard.

The ball may be cleaned when lifted under Rule 24-2b.

(Ball rolling to a position where there is interference by the condition from which relief was taken – ee Rule 20-2c(v).)

Exception: A player may not obtain relief under Rule 24-2b if (a) it is clearly unreasonable for him to play a stroke because of interference by anything other than an immovable obstruction or (b) interference by an immovable obstruction would occur only through use of an unnecessarily abnormal stance, swing or direction of play.

Note: If a ball lies in or touches a **water hazard** (including a **lateral water hazard**), the player is not entitled to relief without penalty from interference by an immovable obstruction. The player shall play the ball as it lies or proceed under Rule 26-1.

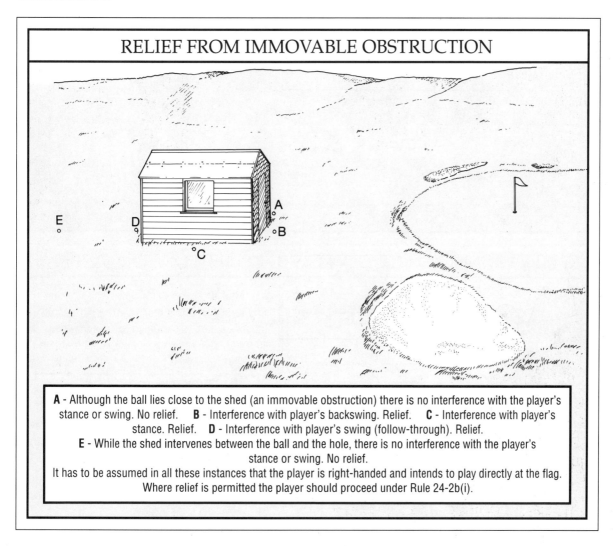

RELIEF FROM IMMOVABLE OBSTRUCTION

A - Although the ball lies close to the shed (an immovable obstruction) there is no interference with the player's stance or swing. No relief.   **B** - Interference with player's backswing. Relief.   **C** - Interference with player's stance. Relief.   **D** - Interference with player's swing (follow-through). Relief.
E - While the shed intervenes between the ball and the hole, there is no interference with the player's stance or swing. No relief.
It has to be assumed in all these instances that the player is right-handed and intends to play directly at the flag. Where relief is permitted the player should proceed under Rule 24-2b(i).

Except in a **water hazard** or a **lateral water hazard**, if there is reasonable evidence that a ball is lost in an immovable obstruction, the player may, without penalty, substitute another ball and follow the procedure prescribed in Rule 24-2b. For the purpose of applying this Rule, the ball shall be deemed to lie at the spot where it entered the obstruction. If the ball is lost in an underground drain pipe or culvert the entrance to which is in a **hazard**, a ball must be dropped in that hazard or the player may proceed under Rule 26-1, if applicable.

C *Ball Lost*

PENALTY FOR BREACH OF RULE: *Match Play – Loss of hole; Stroke play – Two strokes.*

IMMOVABLE OBSTRUCTION

RELIEF FROM OBSTRUCTION GIVES RELIEF FOR LINE OF PLAY

STILE IN BOUNDARY FENCE

NO RELIEF WITHOUT PENALTY IN WATER HAZARD

BALL ON BRIDGE ABOVE HAZARD

The ball is in the water hazard because the margins of a water hazard are deemed to extend vertically upwards. The bridge is an immovable obstruction but there is no relief without penalty from an immovable obstruction when the ball lies in or touches a water hazard. If the ball is played from the bridge the club may be grounded.

GROUND UNDER REPAIR; EXAMPLES

A fallen tree still attached to its stump is not G.U.R., but it can be so declared by the Committee.

A chopped tree trunk is material piled for removal and is G.U.R.

Cracks in the earth are not G.U.R., but the Committee would be justified in declaring a large crack G.U.R.

A rut made by a tractor is not G.U.R., but the Committee would be justified in declaring a deep rut to be G.U.R.

ABNORMAL GROUND CONDITIONS

AND WRONG PUTTING GREEN

Definitions

"Casual water" is any temporary accumulation of water on the **course** which is visible before or after the player takes his **stance** and is not in a **water hazard**. Snow and natural ice, other than frost, are casual water or **loose impediments**, at the option of the player. Manufactured ice is an **obstruction**. Dew and frost are not casual water.

"Ground under repair" is any portion of the **course** so marked by order of the Committee or so declared by its authorised representative. It includes material piled for removal and a hole made by a greenkeeper, even if not so marked. Stakes and lines defining ground under repair are in such ground. The margin of ground under repair extends vertically downwards, but not upwards.

Note 1: Grass cuttings and other material left on the course which have been abandoned and are not intended to be removed are not ground under repair unless so marked.

Note 2: The Committee may make a Local Rule prohibiting play from ground under repair.

Casual Water, Ground Under Repair and Certain Damage to Course   **Rule 25-1**

Interference by **casual water**, **ground under repair** or a hole, cast or runway made by a burrowing animal, a reptile or a bird occurs when a ball lies in or touches any of these conditions or when such a condition on the **course** interferes with the player's **stance** or the area of his intended swing.

a *Interference*

If the player's ball lies on the **putting green**, interference also occurs if such condition on the putting green intervenes on his line of putt.

If interference exists, the player may either play the ball as it lies (unless prohibited by Local Rule) or take relief as provided in Clause b.

If the player elects to take relief, he shall proceed as follows:

b *Relief*

(i)   **Through the Green:** If the ball lies **through the green**, the point on the **course** nearest to where the ball lies shall be determined which (a) is not nearer the hole, (b) avoids interference by the condition, and (c) is not in a **hazard** or on a **putting green**. The player shall lift the ball and drop it without penalty within one club-length of the point thus determined on ground which fulfils (a), (b) and (c) above.

(ii) **In a Hazard:** If the ball lies in or touches a **hazard**, the player shall lift and drop the ball either:

(a) Without penalty, in the hazard, as near as possible to the spot where the ball lay, but not nearer the hole, on ground which affords maximum available relief from the condition; or

71

(b) *Under penalty of one stroke,* outside the hazard, keeping the point where the ball lay directly between the hole and the spot on which the ball is dropped.

Exception: If a ball lies in or touches a **water hazard** (including a **lateral water hazard**), the player is not entitled to relief without penalty from a hole, cast or runway made by a burrowing animal, a reptile or a bird. The player shall play the ball as it lies or proceed under Rule 26-1.

(iii) **On the Putting Green:** If the ball lies on the **putting green,** the player shall lift the ball and place it without penalty in the nearest position to where it lay which affords maximum available relief from the condition, but not nearer the hole nor in a **hazard**.

The ball may be cleaned when lifted under Rule 25-1b.

(Ball rolling to a position where there is interference by the condition from which relief was taken — see Rule 20-2c(v).)

Exception: A player may not obtain relief under Rule 25-1b if (a) it is clearly unreasonable for him to play a stroke because of interference by anything other than a condition covered by Rule 25-1a or (b) interference by such a condition would occur only through use of an unnecessarily abnormal stance, swing or direction of play.

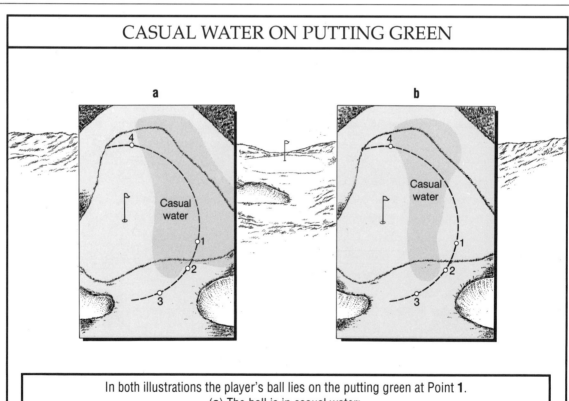

CASUAL WATER ON PUTTING GREEN

In both illustrations the player's ball lies on the putting green at Point **1**.
(**a**) The ball is in casual water;
(**b**) casual water intervenes on the player's line of putt.
In either case, if relief is required, the player must place the ball at Point **3**, the nearest point of 'maximum available relief, even though this is not on the putting green.'

CASUAL WATER IN BUNKER BUT BALL OUTSIDE

CASUAL WATER INTERFERING WITH STANCE

STANCE INTERFERED WITH BY BURROWING ANIMAL HOLE
Ball unplayable because of other condition

My ball is clearly unplayable in the roots of this tree. Can I take free relief because I would have to stand on a rabbit scrape to play it?

No. I'm afraid not. You will have to deem it unplayable under penalty of one shot. You are not entitled to take a free drop by reason of your stance on a rabbit scrape because it is clearly unreasonable for you to play a stroke at your ball where it is lying.

c *Ball Lost Under Condition Covered by Rule 25-1*

It is a question of fact whether a ball lost after having been struck toward a condition covered by Rule 25-1 is lost under such condition. In order to treat the ball as lost under such condition, there must be reasonable evidence to that effect. In the absence of such evidence, the ball must be treated as a lost ball and Rule 27 applies.

(i) **Outside a Hazard:** If a ball is lost outside a **hazard** under a condition covered by Rule 25-1, the player may take relief as follows: the point on the **course** nearest to where the ball last crossed the margin of the area shall be determined which (a) is not nearer the hole than where the ball last crossed the margin, (b) avoids interference by the condition and (c) is not in a hazard or on a **putting green**. He shall drop a ball without penalty within one club-length of the point thus determined on ground which fulfils (a), (b) and (c) above.

(ii) **In a Hazard:** If a ball is lost in a **hazard** under a condition covered by Rule 25-1, the player may drop a ball either:
(a) Without penalty, in the hazard, as near as possible to the point at which the original ball last crossed the margin of the area, but not nearer the hole, on ground which affords maximum available relief from the condition; or
(b) *Under penalty of one stroke*, outside the hazard, keeping the point at which the original ball last crossed the margin of the hazard directly between the hole and the spot on which the ball is dropped.

Exception: If a ball lies in a **water hazard** (including a **lateral water hazard**), the player is not entitled to relief without penalty for a ball lost in a hole, cast or runway made by a burrowing animal, a reptile or a bird. The player shall proceed under Rule 26-1.

Embedded Ball   Rule 25-2

A ball embedded in its own pitch-mark in the ground in any closely-mown area **through the green** may be lifted, cleaned and dropped, without penalty, as near as possible to the spot where it lay but not nearer the hole. "Closely-mown area" means any area of the **course**, including paths through the rough, cut to fairway height or less.

Wrong Putting Green   Rule 25-3

A player must not play a ball which lies on a **putting green** other than that of the hole being played. The ball must be lifted and the player must proceed as follows: The point on the course nearest to where the ball lies shall be determined which (a) is not nearer the hole and (b) is not in a **hazard** or on a putting green. The player shall lift the ball and drop it without penalty within one club-length of the point thus determined on ground which fulfils (a) and (b) above. The ball may be cleaned when so lifted.

Note: Unless otherwise prescribed by the Committee, the term "a putting green other than that of the hole being played" includes a practice putting green or pitching green on the course.

PENALTY FOR BREACH OF RULE: *Match play – Loss of hole; Stroke play – Two strokes*

A ball lies on a wrong putting green and the point on the course nearest to which the ball lies which is not nearer the hole, and is not in a hazard or on a putting green, is point **A**. The player must drop his ball within one club-length of point **A** (shaded area) not nearer the hole.

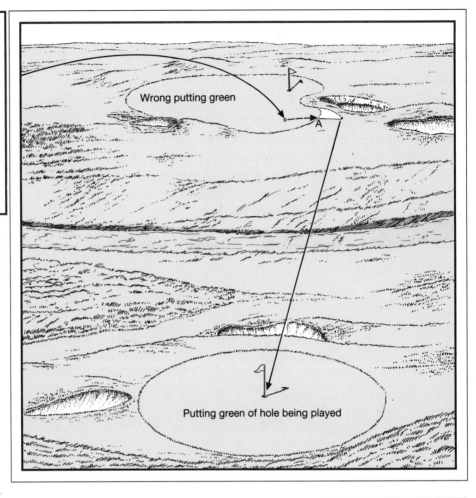

Wrong putting green

A

Putting green of hole being played

WATER HAZARDS

(INCLUDING LATERAL WATER HAZARDS)

Definitions

A "water hazard" is any sea, lake, pond, river, ditch, surface drainage ditch or other open water course (whether or not containing water) and anything of a similar nature.

All ground or water within the margin of a water hazard is part of the water hazard. The margin of a water hazard extends vertically upwards and downwards. Stakes and lines defining the margins of water hazards are in the hazards.

Note: Water hazards (other than **lateral water hazards**) should be defined by yellow stakes or lines.

A "lateral water hazard" is a **water hazard** or that part of a water hazard so situated that it is not possible or is deemed by the Committee to be impracticable to drop a ball behind the water hazard in accordance with Rule 26-1b.

That part of a water hazard to be played as a lateral water hazard should be distinctively marked.

Note: Lateral water hazards should be defined by red stakes or lines.

It is a question of fact whether a ball lost after having been struck towards a **water hazard** is lost inside or outside the hazard. In order to treat the ball as lost in the hazard, there must be reasonable evidence that the ball lodged in it. In the absence of such evidence, the ball must be treated as a lost ball and Rule 27 applies.

If a ball lies in, touches or is lost in a water hazard (whether the ball lies in water or not), the player may *under penalty of one stroke:*

a. Play a ball as nearly as possible at the spot from which the original ball was last played (see Rule 20-5); or

b. Drop a ball behind the water hazard, keeping the point at which the original ball last crossed the margin of the water hazard directly between the hole and the spot on which the ball is dropped, with no limit to how far behind the water hazard the ball may be dropped; or

BALL CROSSING MARGIN OF WATER HAZARD

My ball has crossed the water hazard, but has spun back into it. Where do I take relief?

Under penalty of one stroke, you may either play a ball from where you last played (Rule 26-1a) or you may drop a ball on an extension of the line between the hole and the point at which the ball last crossed the margin (point **B**; Rule 26-1b). The point at which the ball first crossed the margin (point **A**) is irrelevant.

c. *As additional options available only if the ball lies in, touches or is lost in a lateral water hazard,* drop a ball outside the water hazard within two club-lengths of (i) the point where the original ball last crossed the margin of the water hazard or (ii) a point on the opposite margin of the water hazard equidistant from the hole. The ball must be dropped and come to rest not nearer the hole than the point where the original ball last crossed the margin of the water hazard.

The ball may be cleaned when lifted under this Rule.

(Ball moving in water in a water hazard — see Rule 14-6.)

RELIEF FROM LATERAL WATER HAZARD

The player has played a ball from the tee (Point **A**) into the lateral water hazard at Point **B**. It last crossed the margin of the hazard at Point **C** and the point on the opposite margin, equidistant from the hole is Point **E**. He may play the ball as it lies or, under penalty of one stroke:

(**a**) play another ball from the tee - Rule 26-1a;

(**b**) drop a ball anywhere on the far side of the hazard on the dotted line from the hole through point **C**, e.g. Point **D** - Rule 26-1b;

(**c**) drop a ball in the area on the near side of the hazard which is all ground within two club-lengths of Point **C**, but not nearer the hole than Point **C** - Rule 26-1c(i); or

(**d**) drop a ball in the area on the far side of the hazard which is all ground within two club-lengths of Point **E** - Rule 26-1c(ii).

Rule 26-2   **Ball Played Within Water Hazard**

a *Ball Comes to Rest in Hazard*

If a ball played from within a water hazard comes to rest in the hazard after the stroke, the player may:

(i)   proceed under Rule 26-1; or.

(ii)   *under penalty of one stroke,* play a ball as nearly as possible at the spot from which the last stroke from outside the hazard was played (see Rule 20-5).

If the player proceeds under Rule 26-1a, he may elect not to play the dropped ball. If he so elects, he may:

(a) Proceed under Rule 26-1b, *adding the additional penalty of one stroke* prescribed by that Rule; or

(b) Proceed under Rule 26-1c, if applicable, *adding the additional penalty of one stroke* prescribed by that Rule; or

(c) *Add an additional penalty of one stroke* and play a ball as nearly as possible at the spot from which the last stroke from outside the hazard was played (see Rule 20-5).

If a ball played from within a water hazard is lost or declared unplayable outside the hazard or is out of bounds, the player, after taking *a penalty of one stroke* under Rule 27-1 or 28a, may:

b *Ball Lost or Unplayable Outside Hazard or Out of Bounds*

(i) play a ball as nearly as possible at the spot in the hazard from which the original ball was last played (see Rule 20-5); or

(ii) proceed under Rule 26-1b, or if applicable Rule 26-1c, *adding the additional penalty of one stroke* prescribed by the Rule and using as the reference point the point where the original ball last crossed the margin of the hazard before it came to rest in the hazard; or

(iii) *add an additional penalty of one stroke* and play a ball as nearly as possible at the spot from which the last stroke from outside the hazard was played (see Rule 20-5).

Note 1: When proceeding under Rule 26-2b, the player is not required to drop a ball under Rule 27-1 or 28a. If he does drop a ball, he is not required to play it. He may alternatively proceed under Clause (ii) or (iii).

Note 2: If a ball played from within a water hazard is declared unplayable outside the hazard, nothing in Rule 26-2b precludes the player from proceeding under Rule 28b or c.

PENALTY FOR BREACH OF RULE: *Match play – Loss of hole; Stroke play – Two strokes.*

BALL LOST OR OUT OF BOUNDS;
PROVISIONAL BALL

If the original ball is lost in an immovable obstruction (Rule 24-2) or under a condition covered by Rule 25-1 (casual water, ground under repair and certain damage to the course), the player may proceed under the applicable Rule. If the original ball is lost in a water hazard, the player shall proceed under Rule 26.

Such Rules may not be used unless there is reasonable evidence that the ball is lost in an immovable obstruction, under a condition covered by Rule 25-1 or in a water hazard.

Definitions

A ball is "lost" if:

a. It is not found or identified as his by the player within five minutes after the player's side or his or their caddies have begun to search for it; or

b. The player has put another ball into play under the Rules, even though he may not have searched for the original ball; or

c. The player has played any stroke with a **provisional ball** *from the place where the original ball is likely to be or from a point nearer the hole than that place, whereupon the provisional ball becomes the* **ball in play**.

Time spent in playing a **wrong ball** *is not counted in the five-minute period allowed for search.*

"Out of bounds" is ground on which play is prohibited.

When out of bounds is defined by reference to stakes or a fence, or as being beyond stakes or a fence, the out of bounds line is determined by the nearest inside points of the stakes or fence posts at ground level, excluding angled supports.

When out of bounds is defined by a line on the ground, the line itself is out of bounds.

The out of bounds line extends vertically upwards and downwards.

A ball is out of bounds when all of it lies out of bounds.

A player may stand out of bounds to play a ball lying within bounds.

A "provisional ball" is a ball played under Rule 27-2 for a ball which may be **lost** *outside a* **water hazard** *or may be* **out of bounds**.

BALL FOUND WITHIN FIVE MINUTES

Thanks for finding my ball and calling me back before I played another ball. We hadn't been looking for it for five minutes, so I'll just play it.

That's O.K. Your ball wasn't "lost" merely because you went back to play another before the five minutes of search was up. But if you had dropped or played another ball before I called you back that would have become the ball in play and this one would have been "lost". In that situation you couldn't have played on with it.

Ball Lost or Out of Bounds **Rule 27-1**

If a ball is **lost** outside a **water hazard** or is **out of bounds**, the player shall play a ball, *under penalty of one stroke*, as nearly as possible at the spot from which the original ball was last played (see Rule 20-5).

PENALTY FOR BREACH OF RULE 27-1: *Match play – Loss of hole; Stroke play – Two strokes.*

Rule 27-2   Provisional Ball

a *Procedure*

If a ball may be **lost** outside a **water hazard** or may be **out of bounds,** to save time the player may play another ball provisionally as nearly as possible at the spot from which the original ball was played (see Rule 20-5). The player shall inform his opponent in match play or his marker or a fellow-competitor in stroke play that he intends to play a **provisional ball**, and he shall play it before he or his partner goes forward to search for the original ball. If he fails to do so and plays another ball, such ball is not a provisional ball and becomes the **ball in play** *under penalty of stroke and distance* (Rule 27-1); the original ball is deemed to be lost.

b *When Provisional Ball Becomes Ball in Play*

The player may play a provisional ball until he reaches the place where the original ball is likely to be. If he plays a stroke with the provisional ball from the place where the original ball is likely to be or from a point nearer the hole than that place, the original ball is deemed to be **lost** and the provisional ball becomes the ball in play under *penalty of stroke and distance* (Rule 27-1).

If the original ball is lost outside a water hazard or is out of bounds, the provisional ball becomes the ball in play, *under penalty of stroke and distance* (Rule 27-1).

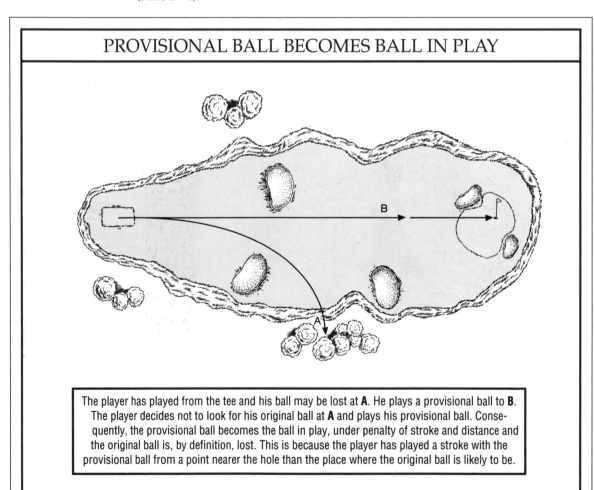

PROVISIONAL BALL BECOMES BALL IN PLAY

The player has played from the tee and his ball may be lost at **A**. He plays a provisional ball to **B**. The player decides not to look for his original ball at **A** and plays his provisional ball. Consequently, the provisional ball becomes the ball in play, under penalty of stroke and distance and the original ball is, by definition, lost. This is because the player has played a stroke with the provisional ball from a point nearer the hole than the place where the original ball is likely to be.

If the original ball is neither lost outside a water hazard nor out of bounds, the player shall abandon the provisional ball and continue play with the original ball. If he fails to do so, any further strokes played with the provisional ball shall constitute playing a **wrong ball** and the provisions of Rule 15 shall apply.

Note: If the original ball lies in a water hazard, the player shall play the ball as it lies or proceed under Rule 26. If it is lost in a water hazard or unplayable, the player shall proceed under Rule 26 or 28, whichever is applicable.

c *When Provisional Ball to Be Abandoned*

PROVISIONAL BALL PLAYED: ORIGINAL BALL FOUND UNPLAYABLE

The ball may be lost in the bushes and the player plays a provisional ball. The original ball is found unplayable, within five minutes and before the provisional ball has become the ball in play. The player must abandon the provisional ball and proceed with the original ball, adopting one of the options under Rule 28.

28

BALL UNPLAYABLE

The player may declare his ball unplayable at any place on the course except when the ball lies in or touches a **water hazard**. The player is the sole judge as to whether his ball is unplayable.

If the player deems his ball to be unplayable, he shall, *under penalty of one stroke:*

a. Play a ball as nearly as possible at the spot from which the original ball was last played (see Rule 20-5); or

b. Drop a ball within two club-lengths of the spot where the ball lay, but not nearer the hole; or

c. Drop a ball behind the point where the ball lay, keeping that point directly between the hole and the spot on which the ball is dropped, with no limit to how far behind that point the ball may be dropped.

If the unplayable ball lies in a **bunker**, the player may proceed under Clause a, b or c. If he elects to proceed under Clause b or c, a ball must be dropped in the bunker.

The ball may be cleaned when lifted under this Rule.

PENALTY FOR BREACH OF RULE: *Match play – Loss of hole; Stroke play – Two strokes.*

The player's tee shot comes to rest in a large bunker, in an unplayable position. Under penalty of one stroke, he has three options under Rule 28:
(**a**) play from where he last played (the tee), or
(**b**) drop a ball in the bunker within two club-lengths of where his ball lay (**A**) but not nearer the hole - i.e. in the indicated area; or
(**c**) drop a ball in the bunker behind the point where the ball lay (**A**), keeping that point directly between the hole and the spot on which the ball is dropped - i.e. line **A-B**.

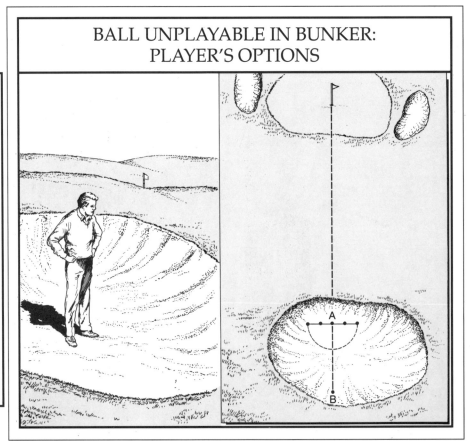

BALL UNPLAYABLE IN BUNKER: PLAYER'S OPTIONS

BALL UNPLAYABLE IN BUSH: PLACE FOR DROPPING

BALL DEEMED UNPLAYABLE

FOURSOMES: ORDER OF PLAY WHEN PARTNER PLAYS OUT OF BOUNDS

No, it's my turn to play. I'll have to play three from the tee. Do I play from the ladies' tee?

No, you must play from the men's tee because that's where the last shot of your side was played from.

That's miles out of bounds. What happens now in mixed four-somes? Do I play again?

ORDER OF PLAY
IN 36-HOLE COMPETITIONS

Now that we're starting the second 18 holes, are we allowed to change the order of teeing off so that you drive at the evens and I drive at the odds?

Yes, unless the Committee in charge of the competition has laid down a condition to the contrary.

Rule 29-1. See Definition of Stipulated Round

FOURSOMES:
WHICH PARTNER DROPS BALL

We are entitled to free relief from the casual water. Do I drop the ball or do you?

It's my turn to play the next shot so I drop the ball.

See Rule 20-2a which requires a ball to be dropped by the player himself.

29

THREESOMES AND FOURSOMES

Definitions

Threesome: A match in which one plays against two, and each side plays one ball.
Foursome: A match in which two play against two, and each side plays one ball.

General   Rule 29-1

In a threesome or a foursome, during any **stipulated round** the partners shall play alternately from the teeing grounds and alternately during the play of each hole. **Penalty strokes** do not affect the order of play.

Match Play   Rule 29-2

If a player plays when his partner should have played, *his side shall lose the hole.*

Stroke Play   Rule 29-3

If the partners play a stroke or strokes in incorrect order, such stroke or strokes shall be cancelled and *the side shall incur a penalty of two strokes.* The side shall correct the error by playing a ball in correct order as nearly as possible at the spot from which it first played in incorrect order (see Rule 20-5). If the side plays a stroke from the next **teeing ground** without first correcting the error or, in the case of the last hole of the round, leaves the **putting green** without declaring its intention to correct the error, *the side shall be disqualified.*

30

THREE-BALL, BEST-BALL

AND FOUR-BALL MATCH PLAY

Definitions

Three-Ball: A match play competition in which three play against one another, each playing his own ball. Each player is playing two distinct matches.
Best-Ball: A match in which one plays against the better ball of two or the best ball of three players.
Four-Ball: A match in which two play their better ball against the better ball of two other players.

Rules of Golf Apply   Rule 30-1

The Rules of Golf, so far as they are not at variance with the following special Rules, shall apply to three-ball, best-ball and four-ball matches.

Rule 30-2 Three-Ball Match Play

a *Ball at Rest Moved by an Opponent*

Except as otherwise provided in the Rules, if the player's ball is touched or moved by an opponent, his **caddie** or **equipment** other than during search, Rule 18-3b applies. *That opponent shall incur a penalty stroke in his match with the player,* but not in his match with the other opponent.

b *Ball Deflected or Stopped by an Opponent Accidentally*

If a player's ball is accidentally deflected or stopped by an opponent, his **caddie** or **equipment**, no penalty shall be incurred. In his match with that opponent the player may play the ball as it lies or, before another stroke is played by either side, he may cancel the stroke and play a ball without penalty as nearly as possible at the spot from which the original ball was last played (see Rule 20-5). In his match with the other opponent, the ball shall be played as it lies.
Exception: Ball striking person attending flagstick — see Rule 17-3b.
(Ball purposely deflected or stopped by an opponent — see Rule 1-2.).

Rule 30-3 Best-Ball and Four-Ball Match Play

a *Representation of Side*

A side may be represented by one partner for all or any part of a match; all partners need not be present. An absent partner may join a match between holes, but not during play of a hole.

b *Maximum of 14 Clubs*

The side shall be penalised for a breach of Rule 4-4 by any partner.

BREACH OF RULE BY ONE PARTNER IN MATCH PLAY

I'll just remove this twig.

I'm afraid you're disqualified from the hole for removing a loose impediment from the bunker. Fortunately, although I'm in the same bunker I'm not penalised because your breach of a rule did not assist my play.

Balls belonging to the same side may be played in the order the side considers best.   **c** *Order of Play*

If a player plays a stroke with a **wrong ball** except in a **hazard**, *he shall be disqualifed*   **d** *Wrong Ball*
for that hole, but his partner incurs no penalty even if the wrong ball belongs to
him. If the wrong ball belongs to another player, its owner shall place a ball on the
spot from which the wrong ball was first played.

(i)   *A side shall be disqualifed* for a breach of any of the following by any partner: **e** *Disqualification*
    Rule 1-3   Agreement to Waive Rules.   *of Side*
    Rule 4-1,-2 or -3 Clubs.
    Rule 5-1, or -2   The Ball.
    Rule 6-2a   Handicap (playing off higher handicap).
    Rule 6-4   Caddie.
    Rule 6-7   Undue Delay (repeated offence).
    Rule 14-3   Artificial Devices and Unusual Equipment.
(ii) *A side shall be disqualifed* for a breach of any of the following by all partners:
    Rule 6-3   Time of Starting and Groups.
    Rule 6-8   Discontinuance of Play.

If a player's breach of a Rule assists his partner's play or adversely affects an   **f** *Effect of Other*
opponent's play, *the partner incurs the applicable penalty in addition to any penalty*   *Penalties*
incurred by the player.

    In all other cases where a player incurs a penalty for breach of a Rule, the
penalty shall not apply to his partner. Where the penalty is stated to be loss of
hole, the effect shall be to disqualify the player for that hole.

g *Another Form of Match Played Concurrently*

In a best-ball or four-ball match when another form of match is played concurrently, the above special Rules shall apply.

31

FOUR-BALL STROKE PLAY

Definitions

In four-ball stroke play two competitors play as partners, each playing his own ball. The lower score of the partners is the score for the hole. If one partner fails to complete the play of the hole, there is no penalty.

Rule 31-1   Rules of Golf Apply

The Rules of Golf, so far as they are not at variance with the following special Rules, shall apply to four-ball stroke play.

Rule 31-2   Representation of Side

A side may be represented by either partner for all or any part of a **stipulated round**; both partners need not be present. An absent competitor may join his partner between holes, but not during play of a hole.

Rule 31-3   Maximum of Fourteen Clubs

The side shall be penalised for a breach of Rule 4-4 by either partner.

Rule 31-4   Scoring

The marker is required to record for each hole only the gross score of whichever partner's score is to count. The gross scores to count must be individually identifiable; otherwise *the side shall be disqualifed*. Only one of the partners need be responsible for complying with Rule 6-6b.

(Wrong score — see Rule 31-7a.)

Rule 31-5   Order of Play

Balls belonging to the same side may be played in the order the side considers best.

Rule 31-6   Wrong Ball

If a competitor plays a stroke with a **wrong ball** except in a **hazard**, *he shall add two penalty strokes to his score for the hole* and shall then play the correct ball. His partner incurs no penalty even if the wrong ball belongs to him.

If the wrong ball belongs to another competitor, its owner shall place a ball on the spot from which the wrong ball was first played.

FOUR-BALL STROKE PLAY.
PARTNER'S SCORES TO BE INDIVIDUALLY IDENTIFIED

Date _3RD APRIL 1992_

Competition _SPRING OPEN FOUR-BALL_

PLAYER A _J. SUTHERLAND_   Handicap _18_   Strokes _18_

PLAYER B _W. B. TAYLOR_   Handicap _12_   Strokes _12_

Hole	Length Yards	Par	Stroke Index	Gross Score A	Gross Score B	Net Score A	Net Score B	Won X Lost – Half O	Mar. Score	Hole	Length Yards	Par	Stroke Index	Gross Score A	Gross Score B	Net Score A	Net Score B	Won X Lost – Half O	Mar. Score
1	437	4	4		5		4		4	10	425	4	3		5	4			6
2	320	4	14	4			③		5	11	141	3	17	3		2			3
3	162	3	18	4		4			4	12	476	5	9	6		5			5
4	504	5	7	6	5				5	13	211	3	11	4	4	3			4
5	181	3	16	4	3				4	14	437	4	5		5	4			5
6	443	4	2		5	4			4	15	460	4	1		5	4			5
7	390	4	8	5	4				4	16	176	3	15	4		3			3
8	346	4	12	5	4				5	17	340	4	13		4	4			4
9	340	4	10		4	3			4	18	435	4	6	6		5			5
Out	3123	35				34 5			39	In	3101	34				34			40
										Out	3123	35				34 5			39
										T'tl	6224	69				68 9			79
										Handicap									
										Net Score									

Player's Signature _J. Sutherland_

Marker's Signature _R. J. Painter_

(**1**) The lower score of the partners is the score for the hole (Rule 31).

(**2**) Only one of the partners need be responsible for complying with Rule 6-6b, i.e. recording scores, checking scores, countersigning and returning the card (Rule 31-4).

(**3**) The competitor is solely responsible for the correctness of the gross score recorded. Although there is no objection to the competitor (or his marker) entering the net score, it is the Committee's responsibility to record the better ball score for each hole, to add up the scores and to apply the handicaps recorded on the card (Rule 33-5). Thus there is no penalty for the error in recording the net score at the second hole.

(**4**) Scores of the two partners must be kept in separate columns otherwise it is impossible for the Committee to apply the correct handicap. If the scores of both partners, having different handicaps, are recorded in the same column, the Committee has no alternative but to disqualify both partners (Rules 31-7 and 6-6 apply).

(**5**) There is nothing in the Rules that requires an alteration to be initialled.

(**6**) The Committee is responsible for laying down the conditions under which a competition is to be played (Rule 33-1), including the method of handicapping.

In the above illustration the Committee laid down that full handicaps would apply.

Rule 31-7	**Disqualification Penalties**

a *Breach by One Partner*

A side shall be disqualified from the competition for a breach of any of the following by either partner:

Rule 1-3	Agreement to Waive Rules.
Rule 3-4	Refusal to Comply with Rule.
Rule 4-1,-2 or -3	Clubs.
Rule 5-1 or -2	The Ball.
Rule 6-2b	Handicap (playing off higher handicap; failure to record handicap).
Rule 6-4	Caddie.
Rule 6-6b	Signing and Returning Card.
Rule 6-6d	Wrong Score for Hole, i.e. when the recorded score of the partner whose score is to count is lower than actually taken. If the recorded score of the partner whose score is to count is higher than actually taken, it must stand as returned.
Rule 6-7	Undue Delay (repeated offence).
Rule 7-1	Practice Before or Between Rounds.
Rule 14-3	Artificial Devices and Unusual Equipment.
Rule 31-4	Gross Scores to count Not Individually Identifiable.

b *Breach by Both Partners*

A side shall be disqualified:

(i)   for a breach by both partners of Rule 6-3 (Time of Starting and Groups) or Rule 6-8 (Discontinuance of Play), or

(ii)   if, at the same hole, each partner is in breach of a Rule the penalty for which is disqualification from the competition or for a hole.

c *For the Hole Only*

In all other cases where a breach of a Rule would entail disqualification, *the competitor shall be disqualified only for the hole at which the breach occurred.*

Rule 31-8	**Effect of Other Penalties**

If a competitor's breach of a Rule assists his partner's play, *the partner incurs the applicable penalty in addition to any penalty incurred by the competitor.*

In all other cases where a competitor incurs a penalty for breach of a Rule, the penalty shall not apply to his partner.

32

BOGEY, PAR AND STABLEFORD

COMPETITIONS

Definitions

Bogey, par and Stableford competitions are forms of stroke competition in which play is against a fixed score at each hole. The Rules for stroke play, so far as they are not at variance with the following special Rules, apply.

Conditions — Rule 32-1

The reckoning for bogey and par competitions is made as in match play. Any hole for which a competitor makes no return shall be regarded as a loss. The winner is the competitor who is most successful in the aggregate of holes.

a *Bogey and Par Competitions*

The marker is responsible for marking only the gross number of strokes for each hole where the competitor makes a net score equal to or less than the fixed score.
Note: Maximum of 14 Clubs – Penalties as in match play – see Rule 4-4.

The reckoning in Stableford competitions is made by points awarded in relation to a fixed score at each hole as follows:

b *Stableford Competitions*

Hole Played in	Points
More than one over fixed score or no score returned 0	
One over fixed score 1	
Fixed Score 2	
One under fixed score 3	
Two under fixed score 4	
Three under fixed score 5	
Four under fixed score 6	

The winner is the competitor who scores the highest number of points.

The marker shall be responsible for marking only the gross number of strokes at each hole where the competitor's net score earns one or more points.
Note: Maximum of 14 Clubs (Rule 4-4) – Penalties applied as follows: From total points scored for the round, deduction of two points for each hole at which any breach occurred; maximum deduction per round: four points.

Disqualification Penalties — Rule 32-2

A competitor shall be disqualifed from the competition for a breach of any of the following:

a *From the Competition*

Rule 1-3	Agreement to Waive Rules.
Rule 3-4	Refusal to Comply with Rule.
Rule 4-1, -2 or -3	Clubs.
Rule 5-1 or -2	The Ball.
Rule 6-2b	Handicap (playing off higher handicap; failure to record handicap).
Rule 6-3	Time of Starting and Groups.
Rule 6-4	Caddie.
Rule 6-6b	Signing and Returning Card.
Rule 6-6d	Wrong Score for Hole, except that no penalty shall be incurred when a breach of this Rule does not affect the result of the hole.
Rule 6-7	Undue Delay (repeated offence).
Rule 6-8	Discontinuance of Play.
Rule 7-1	Practice Before or Between Rounds.
Rule 14-3	Artificial Devices and Unusual Equipment.

In all other cases where a breach of a Rule would entail disqualification, *the competitor shall be disqualified only for the hole at which the breach occurred.*

b *For a Hole*

93

THE COMMITTEE

| **Rule 33-1** | **Conditions; Waiving Rule** |

The Committee shall lay down the conditions under which a competition is to be played.

The Committee has no power to waive a Rule of Golf.

Certain special rules governing stroke play are so substantially different from those governing match play that combining the two forms of play is not practicable and is not permitted. The results of matches played and the scores returned in these circumstances shall not be accepted.

In stroke play the Committee may limit a referee's duties.

| **Rule 33-2** | **The Course** |

a *Defining Bounds and Margins*

The Committee shall define accurately:
 (i)   the **course** and **out of bounds**,
 (ii) the margins of **water hazards** and **lateral water hazards**,
 (iii) **ground under repair**, and
 (iv)   **obstructions** and integral parts of the course.

b *New Holes*

New holes should be made on the day on which a stroke competition begins and at such other times as the Committee considers necessary, provided all competitors in a single round play with each hole cut in the same position.
Exception: When it is impossible for a damaged hole to be repaired so that it conforms with the Definition, the Committee may make a new hole in a nearby similar position.

c *Practice Ground*

Where there is no practice ground available outside the area of a competition **course**, the Committee should lay down the area on which players may practise on any day of a competition, if it is practicable to do so. On any day of a stroke competition, the Committee should not normally permit practice on or to a **putting green** or from a **hazard** of the competition course.

d *Course Unplayable*

If the Committee or its authorised representative considers that for any reason the course is not in a playable condition, or that there are circumstances which render the proper playing of the game impossible, it may, in match play or stroke play, order a temporary suspension of play or, in stroke play, declare play null and void and cancel all scores for the round in question. When play has been temporarily suspended, it shall be resumed from where it was discontinued, even though resumption occurs on a subsequent day. When a round is cancelled, all penalties incurred in that round are cancelled.

(Procedure in discontinuing play — see Rule 6-8.)

Times of Starting and Groups   Rule 33-3

The Committee shall lay down the times of starting and, in stroke play, arrange the groups in which competitors shall play.

When a match play competition is played over an extended period, the Committee shall lay down the limit of time within which each round shall be completed. When players are allowed to arrange the date of their match within these limits, the Committee should announce that the match must be played at a stated time on the last day of the period unless the players agree to a prior date.

Handicap Stroke Table   Rule 33-4

The Committee shall publish a table indicating the order of holes at which handicap strokes are to be given or received.

Score Card   Rule 33-5

In stroke play, the Committee shall issue for each competitor a score card containing the date and the competitor's name or, in foursome or four-ball stroke play, the competitors' names.

In stroke play, the Committee is responsible for the addition of scores and application of the handicap recorded on the card.

In four-ball stroke play, the Committee is responsible for recording the better-ball score for each hole and in the process applying the handicaps recorded on the card, and adding the better-ball scores.

In bogey, par and Stableford competitions, the Committee is responsible for applying the handicap recorded on the card and determining the result of each hole and the overall result or points total.

Decision of Ties   Rule 33-6

The Committee shall announce the manner, day and time for the decision of a halved match or of a tie, whether played on level terms or under handicap.

A halved match shall not be decided by stroke play. A tie in stroke play shall not be decided by a match.

Disqualification Penalty; Committee Discretion   Rule 33-7

A penalty of disqualification may in exceptional individual cases be waived, modified or imposed if the Committee considers such action warranted.

Any penalty less than disqualification shall not be waived or modified.

Local Rules   Rule 33-8

The Committee may make and publish Local Rules for abnormal conditions if they are consistent with the policy of the Governing Authority for the country concerned as set forth in Appendix I to these Rules.

a *Policy*

A penalty imposed by a Rule of Golf shall not be waived by a Local Rule.

b *Waiving Penalty*

DISPUTES AND DECISIONS

Rule 34-1   Claims and Penalties

a *Match Play*

In match play if a claim is lodged with the Committee under Rule 2-5, a decision should be given as soon as possible so that the state of the match may, if necessary, be adjusted.

If a claim is not made within the time limit provided by Rule 2-5, it shall not be considered unless it is based on facts previously unknown to the player making the claim and the player making the claim had been given wrong information (Rules 6-2a and 9) by an opponent. In any case, no later claim shall be considered after the result of the match has been officially announced, unless the Committee is satisfied that the opponent knew he was giving wrong information.

b *Stroke Play*

In stroke play no penalty shall be rescinded, modified or imposed after the competition has closed, except that a *penalty of disqualification* shall be imposed at any time after the competition has closed if a competitor:

(i)   returned a score for any hole lower than actually taken (Rule 6-6d) for any reason other than failure to include a penalty which he did not know he had incurred; or

(ii)   returned a score card on which he had recorded a handicap which he knew was higher than that to which he was entitled, and this affected the number of strokes received (Rule 6-2b); or

(iii) was in breach of Rule 1-3.

A competition is deemed to have closed when the result has been officially announced or, in stroke play qualifying followed by match play, when the player has teed off in his first match.

Rule 34-2   Referee's Decision

If a referee has been appointed by the Committee, his decision shall be final.

Rule 34-3   Committee's Decision

In the absence of a referee, any dispute or doubtful point on the Rules shall be referred to the Committee, whose decision shall be final.

If the Committee cannot come to a decision, it shall refer the dispute or doubtful point to the Rules of Golf Committee of the Royal and Ancient Golf Club of St. Andrews, whose decision shall be final.

If the dispute or doubtful point has not been referred to the Rules of Golf Committee, the player or players have the right to refer an agreed statement through the Secretary of the Club to the Rules of Golf Committee for an opinion as to the correctness of the decision given. The reply will be sent to the Secretary of the Club or Clubs concerned.

If play is conducted other than in accordance with the Rules of Golf, the Rules of Golf Committee will not give a decision on any question.

APPENDIX I

LOCAL RULES (RULE 33-8) AND CONDITIONS

OF THE COMPETITION (RULE 33-1)

Local Rules   **Part A**

The Committee may make and publish Local Rules (for Specimen Local Rules see Part B) for such abnormal conditions as:

Obstructions   **1**

Clarifying the status of objects which may be obstructions (Rule 24).   **a** *General*

   Declaring any construction to be an integral part of the course and, accordingly, not an obstruction, e.g. built-up sides of teeing grounds, putting greens and bunkers (Rules 24 and 33-2a).

Allowing the removal of stones in bunkers by declaring them to be "movable obstructions" (Rule 24).   **b** *Stones in Bunkers*

(i)   Declaring artificial surfaces and sides of roads and paths to be integral parts of the course, or   **c** *Roads and Paths*

(ii)   Providing relief of the type afforded under Rule 24-2b from roads and paths not having artificial surfaces and sides if they could unfairly affect play.

Providing relief from intervention by fixed sprinkler heads within two club-lengths of the putting green when the ball lies within two club-lengths of the sprinkler head.   **d** *Fixed Sprinkler Heads*

Providing relief for the protection of young trees.   **e** *Protection of Young Trees*

Specimen Local Rules for application in Tournament Play are available from the Royal and Ancient Golf Club of St. Andrews.   **f** *Temporary Immovable Obstructions*

Areas of the Course Requiring Preservation   **2**

Assisting preservation of the course by defining areas, including turf nurseries, young plantations and other parts of the course under cultivation, as "ground under repair" from which play is prohibited.

Unusual Damage to the Course or   **3**
Accumulation of Leaves (or the Like)

Declaring such areas to be "ground under repair" (Rule 25).
Note: For relief from aeration holes see Specimen Local Rule 8 in Part B of this Appendix.

4   Extreme Wetness, Mud, Poor Conditions and Protection of the Course

a *Lifting an Embedded Ball, Cleaning*

Where the ground is unusually soft, the Committee may, by temporary Local Rule, allow the lifting of a ball which is embedded in its own pitch-mark in the ground in an area "through the green" which is not "closely mown" (Rule 25-2) if it is satisfied that the proper playing of the game would otherwise be prevented. The Local Rule shall be for that day only or for a short period, and if practicable shall be confined to specified areas. The Committee shall withdraw the Local Rule as soon as conditions warrant and should not print it on the score card.

In similarly adverse conditions, the Committee may, by temporary Local Rule, permit the cleaning of a ball "through the green".

b *"Preferred Lies" and "Winter Rules"*

Adverse conditions, including the poor condition of the course or the existence of mud, are sometimes so general, particularly during winter months, that the Committee may decide to grant relief by temporary Local Rule either to protect the course or to promote fair and pleasant play. Such Local Rule shall be withdrawn as soon as conditions warrant.

A player is entitled to relief from a fixed sprinkler head (an immovable obstruction) under Rule 24-2.
If the specimen Local Rule is introduced, a player is also entitled to relief for intervention to his line of play provided:
(**a**) the fixed sprinkler head is on or within two club-lengths of the putting green; and
(**b**) the ball lies within two club-lengths of the fixed sprinkler head.

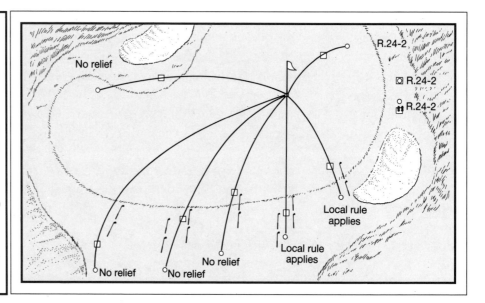

5   Other Local Conditions which Interfere with the Proper Playing of the Game

If this necessitates modification of a Rule of Golf the approval of the Governing Authority must be obtained.

Other matters which the Committee could cover by Local Rule include:

6   Water Hazards

a *Lateral Water Hazards*

Clarifying the status of sections of water hazards which may be lateral water hazards (Rule 26).

   b *Provisional Ball*   Permitting play of a provisional ball for a ball which may be in a water hazard of such character that it would be impracticable to determine whether the ball is in the hazard or to do so would unduly delay play. In such a case, if a provisional ball is played and the original ball is in a water hazard, the player may play the original ball as it lies or continue the provisional ball in play, but he may not proceed under Rule 26-1.

Defining Bounds and Margins   7

Specifying means used to define out of bounds, hazards, water hazards, lateral water hazards and ground under repair.

Dropping Zones   8

Establishing special areas in which balls may or shall be dropped when it is not feasible or practicable to proceed exactly in conformity with Rule 24-2b (Immovable Obstruction), Rule 25-lb or Rule 25-1c (Ground Under Repair), Rule 26-1 (Water Hazards and Lateral Water Hazards) or Rule 28 (Ball Unplayable).

Priority on the Course   9

The Committee may make regulations governing Priority on the Course (see Etiquette).

Specimen Local Rules   Part B

Within the policy set out in Part A of this Appendix the Committee may adopt a Specimen Local Rule by referring, on a score card or notice board, to the examples given below. However Specimen Local Rules 5, 6 or 7 should not be printed or referred to on a score card as they are all of limited duration.

Fixed Sprinkler Heads   1

All fixed sprinkler heads are immovable obstructions and relief from interference by them may be obtained under Rule 24-2. In addition, if such an obstruction on or within two club-lengths of the putting green of the hole being played intervenes on the line of play between the ball and the hole, the player may obtain relief, without penalty, as follows:

If the ball lies off the putting green but not in a hazard and is within two club-lengths of the intervening obstruction, it may be lifted, cleaned and dropped at the nearest point to where the ball lay which (a) is not nearer the hole, (b) avoids such intervention and (c) is not in a hazard or on a putting green.

PENALTY FOR BREACH OF LOCAL RULE: *Match play – Loss of hole; Stroke play – Two strokes.*

Stones in Bunkers   2

Stones in bunkers are movable obstructions (Rule 24-1 applies).

Protection of Young Trees   3

Protection of young trees identified by_____ . If such a tree interferes with a player's stance or the area of his intended swing, the ball must be lifted, without penalty, and dropped in accordance with the procedure prescribed in Rule 24-2b(i) (Immovable Obstruction). The ball may be cleaned when so lifted.

PENALTY FOR BREACH OF LOCAL RULE: *Match play – Loss of hole; Stroke play – Two strokes.*

4   Ground Under Repair: Play Prohibited

If a player's ball lies in an area of "ground under repair" from which play is prohibited, or if such an area of "ground under repair" interferes with the player's stance or the area of his intended swing the player must take relief under Rule 25-1.

PENALTY FOR BREACH OF LOCAL RULE: *Match play – Loss of hole; Stroke play – Two strokes.*

5   Lifting an Embedded Ball

[*Specify the area if practicable*]. . . through the green, a ball embedded in its own pitch-mark in ground other than sand may be lifted, cleaned and dropped, without penalty, as near as possible to the spot where it lay but not nearer the hole.

PENALTY FOR BREACH OF LOCAL RULE: *Match play – Loss of hole; Stroke play – Two strokes.*

6   Cleaning Ball

[*Specify the area if practicable*]. . . through the green a ball may be lifted, cleaned and replaced without penalty.

Note: The position of the ball shall be marked before it is lifted under this Local Rule – see Rule 20-1.

7   "Preferred Lies" and "Winter Rules"

A ball lying on any "closely mown area" through the green may, without penalty, be moved or may be lifted, cleaned and placed within six inches of where it originally lay, but not nearer the hole. After the ball has been so moved or placed, it is in play.

PENALTY FOR BREACH OF LOCAL RULE: *Match play – Loss of hole; Stroke play – Two strokes.*

8   Aeration Holes

If a ball comes to rest in an aeration hole, the player may, without penalty, lift the ball and clean it. Through the green, the player shall drop the ball as near as possible to where it lay, but not nearer the hole. On the putting green, the player shall place the ball at the nearest spot not nearer the hole which avoids such situation.

PENALTY FOR BREACH OF LOCAL RULE: *Match play – Loss of hole; Stroke play – Two strokes.*

Part C   Conditions of the Competition

Rule 33-1 provides, "The Committee shall lay down the conditions under which a competition is to be played". Such conditions should include many matters such as method of entry, eligibility, number of rounds to be played, settling ties, etc. which it is not appropriate to deal with in the Rules of Golf or this Appendix.

However there are four matters which might be covered in the Conditions of the Competition to which the Committee's attention is specifically drawn by way of a Note to the appropriate Rule. These are:

1   Specification of the Ball (Note to Rule 5-1)

Arising from the regulations for ball-testing under Rule 5-1, Lists of Conforming Golf Balls will be issued from time to time.

It is recommended that the Lists should be applied to all National and County (or equivalent) Championships and to all top class events when restricted to low handicap players. In order to apply the Lists to a particular competition the Committee must lay this down in the Conditions of the Competition. This should be referred to in the Entry Form, and also a notice should be displayed on the Club notice board and at the 1st Tee along the following lines:

....[*Name of Event*]...

....[*Date and Club*]...

The ball the player uses shall be named on the current List of Conforming Golf Balls issued by the Royal and Ancient Golf Club of St. Andrews.

Note 1: A penalty statement will be required and must be either:

(a)   "**PENALTY FOR BREACH OF CONDITION**: *Disqualification.*"

or

(b)   "**PENALTY FOR BREACH OF CONDITION**:
Match play – Loss of each hole at which a breach occurred;
Stroke play – Two strokes for each hole at which a breach occurred."

If option (b) is adopted this only applies to use of a ball which, whilst not on the List of Conforming Golf Balls, does conform to the specifications set forth in Rule 5 and Appendix III. The penalty for use of a ball which does not so conform is disqualification.

Note 2: In Club events it is recommended that no such condition be applied.

Time of Starting (Note to Rule 6-3a)   2

If the Committee wishes to act in accordance with the Note, the following wording is recommended:

"If, in the absence of circumstances which warrant waiving the penalty of disqualification as provided in Rule 33-7, the player arrives at his starting point, ready to play, within five minutes after his starting time, the penalty for failure to start on time is loss of the first hole in match play or two strokes at the first hole in stroke play."

Practice   3

The Committee may make regulations governing practice in accordance with the Note to Rule 7-1, Exception (c) to Rule 7-2, Note 2 to Rule 7 and Rule 33-2c.

Advice in Team Competitions   4

If the Committee wishes to act in accordance with the Note, the following wording is recommended:

"In accordance with the Note to Rule 8 of the Rules of Golf each team may appoint one person (in addition to the persons from whom advice may be asked under that Rule) who may give advice to members of that team. Such person [*if it is desired to insert any restriction on who may be nominated, insert such restriction here*] shall be identified to the Committee prior to the start of the competition."

101

APPENDICES II AND III

Any design in a club or ball which is not covered by Rules 4 and 5 and Appendices II and III, or which might significantly change the nature of the game, will be ruled on by the Royal and Ancient Golf Club of St. Andrews and the United States Golf Association. Note: Equipment approved for use or marketed prior to 1st January 1988 which conformed to the Rules in effect in 1987 but does not conform to the 1988 and subsequent Rules may be used until 31st December 1995; thereafter all equipment must conform to the current Rules.

APPENDIX II

DESIGN OF CLUBS

Rule 4-1 prescribes general regulations for the design of clubs. The following paragraphs, which provide some detailed specifications and clarify how Rule 4-1 is interpreted, should be read in conjunction with this Rule.

Rule 4-1a	**General**

Adjustability - Exception for Putters

Clubs other than putters shall not be designed to be adjustable except for weight.
    Some other forms of adjustability are permitted in the design of a putter, provided that:
(i)   the adjustment cannot be readily made;
(ii)   all adjustable parts are firmly fixed and there is no reasonable likelihood of them working loose during a round; and
(iii)   all configurations of adjustment conform with the Rules.
    The disqualification penalty for purposely changing the playing characteristics of a club during a **stipulated round** (Rule 4-2) applies to all clubs including a putter. *Note*: It is recommended that all putters with adjustable parts be submitted to the Royal and Ancient Golf Club of St. Andrews for a ruling.

Rule 4-1b	**Shaft**

Generally Straight

The shaft shall be at least 18 inches (457mm) in length. It shall be straight from the top of the grip to a point not more than 5 inches (127mm) above the sole, measured along the axis of the shaft and the neck or socket.

Bending and Twisting Properties

The shaft must be so designed and manufactured that at any point along its length:
(i)   it bends in such a way that the deflection is the same regardless of how the shaft is rotated about its longitudinal axis; and
(ii)   it twists the same amount in both directions.

Attachment to Clubhead

The neck or socket must not be more than 5 inches (127mm) in length, measured from the top of the neck or socket to the sole along its axis. The shaft and the neck or socket must remain in line with the heel, or with a point to the right or left of the heel, when the club is viewed in the address position. The distance between the axis of the shaft or the neck or socket and the back of the heel must not exceed

0.625 inches (16mm).

Exception for Putters: The shaft or neck or socket of a putter may be fixed at any point in the head and need not remain in line with the heel. The axis of the shaft from the top to a point not more than 5 inches (127mm) above the sole must diverge from the vertical in the toe-heel plane by at least 10 degrees when the club is in its normal address position.

Grip   Rule 4-1c

(i) For clubs other than putters the grip must be generally circular in cross-section, except that a continuous, straight, slightly raised rib may be incorporated along the full length of the grip.

(ii) A putter grip may have a non-circular cross-section, provided the cross-section has no concavity and remains generally similar throughout the length of the grip.

(iii) The grip may be tapered but must not have any bulge or waist.

(iv) For clubs other than putters the axis of the grip must coincide with the axis of the shaft.

(v) The cross-sectional dimension of a grip measured in any direction shall not exceed 1.75 inches (45mm).

(vi) A putter may have more than one grip, provided each is circular in cross-section and the axis of each coincides with the axis of the shaft.

Note: Putters approved for use or marketed prior to 1st January 1992 which are in breach of clause (vi), but otherwise conform, may be used until 31st December 1992.

Clubhead   Rule 4-1d

The dimensions of a clubhead (see diagram) are measured, with the clubhead in its normal address position, on horizontal lines between vertical projections of the outermost points of (i) the heel and the toe and (ii) the face and the back. If the outermost point of the heel is not clearly defined, it is deemed to be 0.625 inches (16mm) above the horizontal plane on which the club is resting in its normal address position.

Dimensions

The clubhead shall be generally plain in shape. All parts shall be rigid, structural in nature and functional.

Features such as holes through the head, windows or transparencies, or appendages to the main body of the head such as plates, rods or fins for the purpose of meeting dimensional specifications, for aiming or for any other purpose are not permitted. Exceptions may be made for putters.

Any furrows in or runners on the sole shall not extend into the face.

Plain in Shape

Club Face   Rule 4-1e

Except for specified markings, the surface roughness must not exceed that of decorative sandblasting. Markings must not have sharp edges or raised lips, as determined by a finger test. The material and construction of the face shall not be designed or manufactured to have the effect at impact of a spring, or to impart significantly more spin to the ball than a standard steel face, or to have any other effect which would unduly influence the movement of the ball.

General

103

"Impact Area" Markings

Markings within the area where impact is intended (the "impact area") are governed by the following:.

(i)   **Grooves** A series of straight grooves with diverging sides and a symmetrical cross-section may be used. (See diagram.) The width and cross-section must be generally consistent across the face of the club and along the length of the grooves. Any rounding of groove edges shall be in the form of a radius which does not exceed 0.020 inches (0.5mm). The width of the grooves shall not exceed 0.035 inches (0.9mm), using the 30 degree method of measurement on file with the Royal and Ancient Golf Club of St. Andrews. The distance between edges of adjacent grooves must not be less than three times the width of a groove, and not less than 0.075 inches (1.9mm). The depth of a groove must not exceed 0.020 inches (0.5mm).

Note: Until 31st December 1995, a Committee is authorised to waive the above requirements for width and separation of grooves for clubs manufactured before 31st March 1990, provided the width of the grooves does not exceed 0.040 inches (1.00mm) and the distance between edges of adjacent grooves is not less than 2.3 times the width.

It is recommended that the granting of this waiver be the normal practice for amateur competition and, in that case, the Committee need not give written intimation that the waiver is being applied.

Where a Committee opts not to grant the waiver and to apply the Rule strictly (as it is entitled to do), this should be clearly stated in the Conditions of the Competition and the Entry Form.

From 1st January 1996, the Rule may no longer be waived and markings on clubs must meet all the specifications of the Rule.

(ii)   **Punch Marks** Punch marks may be used. The area of any such mark must not exceed 0.0044 square inches (2.8 sq.mm). A mark must not be closer to an adjacent mark than 0.168 inches (4.3mm) measured from centre to centre. The depth of a punch mark must not exceed 0.040 inches (1.0mm). If punch marks are used in combination with grooves, a punch mark may not be closer to a groove than 0.168 inches (4.3mm), measured from centre to centre.

Decorative Markings

The centre of the impact area may be indicated by a design within the boundary of a square whose sides are 0.375 inches (9.5mm) in length. Such a design must not unduly influence the movement of the ball. Decorative markings are permitted outside the impact area.

Non-Metallic Club Face Markings

The above specifications do not apply to clubs on which the impact area of the face is non-metallic and whose loft angle is 24 degrees or less, but markings which could unduly influence the movement of the ball are prohibited. Clubs with this type of face and a loft angle exceeding 24 degrees may have grooves of maximum width 0.040 inches (1.0mm) and maximum depth 1½ times the groove width, but must otherwise conform to the markings specifications above.

Putter Face Markings

The specifications above with regard to club face markings do not apply to putters.

CLUBS

Shaft

PUTTER

Neck or socket

Faces

Toe

Face

Heel

Heel

Sole

Toe

Sole

GRIPS

CLUB GRIP   Circular

PUTTER GRIP   Flat side (Permitted on Putters only)

GROOVES

Groove width max. 0.035″

Groove depth max. 0.020″

30°   30°

EXAMPLES OF PERMISSIBLE GROOVE CROSS-SECTIONS

APPENDIX III

THE BALL

a *Weight*

The weight of the ball shall not be greater than 1.620 ounces avoirdupois (45.93g).

b *Size*

The diameter of the ball shall be not less than 1.680 inches (42.67mm). This specification will be satisfied if, under its own weight, a ball falls through a 1.680 inches diameter ring gauge in fewer than 25 out of 100 randomly selected positions, the test being carried out at a temperature of $23 \pm 1°C$.

c *Spherical Symmetry*

The ball must not be designed, manufactured or intentionally modified to have flight properties which differ from those of a spherically symmetrical ball.

Furthermore the ball will not conform to the Rules of Golf if it fails to satisfy the performance specifications outlined below:

As described in procedures on file at the Royal and Ancient Golf Club of St. Andrews, each ball type will be tested using 40 balls of that type, in 20 pairs. One ball of each pair will be launched spinning about one specified axis; the other ball of each pair will be launched spinning about a different, but also specified, axis. Differences in carry and time of flight between the two balls of each pair will be recorded. If the mean of the differences in carry is greater than 3.0 yards, and that value is significant at the 5% level, OR if the mean of the differences in time of flight is greater than 0.20 seconds, and that value is significant at the 5% level, the ball type will not conform to the Rules of Golf.

Note: Methods of determining whether a ball performs as if it were generally spherically symmetrical may be subject to change as instrumentation becomes available to measure other properties accurately, such as the aerodynamic coefficient of lift, coefficient of drag and moment of inertia.

d *Initial Velocity*

The velocity of the ball shall not be greater than 250 feet (76.2m) per second when measured on apparatus approved by the Royal and Ancient Golf Club of St. Andrews. A maximum tolerance of 2% will be allowed. The temperature of the ball when tested shall be $23 \pm 1°C$.

e *Overall Distance Standard*

A brand of golf ball, when tested on apparatus approved by the Royal and Ancient Golf Club of St. Andrews under the conditions set forth in the Overall Distance Standard for golf balls on file with the Royal and Ancient Golf Club of St. Andrews, shall not cover an average distance in carry and roll exceeding 280 yards (256 metres) plus a tolerance of 6%.

Note: The 6% tolerance will be reduced to a minimum of 4% as test techniques are improved.

HANDICAPS

The Rules of Golf do not legislate for the allocation and adjustment of handicaps or their playing differentials. Such matters are within the jurisdiction and control of the National Union concerned and queries should be directed accordingly.

R&A POLICY ON GAMBLING

The Definition of an Amateur Golfer provides that an Amateur golfer is one who plays the game as a non-remunerative or non-profit-making sport. When gambling motives are introduced, evils can arise which threaten the integrity both of the game and of the individual players.

The R&A does not object to participation in wagering among individual golfers or teams of golfers when participation in the wagering is limited to the players, the players may only wager on themselves or their teams, the sole source of all money won by players is advanced by the players and the primary purpose is the playing of the game for enjoyment.

The distinction between playing for prize money and gambling is essential to the validity of the Rules of Amateur Status. The following constitute golf wagering and not playing for prize money:
1 Participation in wagering among individual golfers.
2 Participation in wagering among teams.

Organised Amateur events open to the general golfing public and designed and promoted to create cash prizes are not approved by the R&A. Golfers participating in such events without irrevocably waiving their right to cash prizes are deemed by the R&A to be playing for prize money

The R&A is opposed to and urges Unions and Clubs and all other sponsors of golf competitions to prohibit types of gambling such as: Calcuttas, auction sweepstakes and any other forms of gambling organised for general participation or permitting participants to bet on someone other than themselves or their teams.

Attention is drawn to Rule 1-11 relating to conduct detrimental to the game, under which players can forfeit their Amateur Status. It is the Club which, by permitting competitions where excessive gambling is involved, or illegal prizes are offered, bears the responsibility for which the individual is penalised, and Unions have the power to invoke severe sanctions against a Club or individual for consistently ignoring this policy.

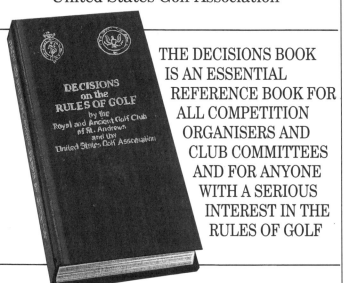